DATE DUE

APR 2 3 2002	
NOV 1 6 2002	
DEC 0 8 2002	
NOV 2 6 2003	

BRODART   Cat. No. 23-221

Helping Athletes

WITH

EATING DISORDERS

Ron A. Thompson, PhD
Roberta Trattner Sherman, PhD
Bloomington Center for Counseling and Human Development
Bloomington, IN

Human Kinetics Publishers

Library of Congress Cataloging-in-Publication Data

Thompson, Ron A.
 Helping athletes with eating disorders / Ron A. Thompson, Roberta
Trattner Sherman.
   p.   cm.
 Includes bibliographical references and index.
 ISBN 0-87322-383-7
 1. Eating disorders--Treatment. 2. Athletes--Nutrition.
3. Athletes--Mental health. I. Sherman, Roberta Trattner, 1949-
II. Title.
 RC552.E18T46   1993
 616.85'26'0088796--dc20   93-17200
                                                                        CIP

ISBN: 0-87322-383-7

Developmental Editor: Mary E. Fowler
Assistant Editors: Moyra Knight, Julie Swadener, and John Wentworth
Copyeditor: Barbara Walsh
Proofreader: Stefani Day
Indexer: Barbara E. Cohen
Production Director: Ernie Noa
Typesetting and Text Layout: Angela K. Snyder
Text Design: Keith Blomberg
Cover Design: Jack Davis
Illustrations: Cynthia Ann Butler
Printer: Braun-Brumfield

Printed in the United States of America

10 9 8 7 6 5 4 3 2 1

Human Kinetics Publishers
Box 5076, Champaign, IL 61825-5076
1-800-747-4457

Canada Office:
Human Kinetics Publishers
P.O. Box 2503, Windsor, ON N8Y 4S2
1-800-465-7301 (in Canada only)

Europe Office:
Human Kinetics Publishers (Europe) Ltd.
P.O. Box IW14
Leeds LS16 6TR
England
0532-781708

Australia Office:
Human Kinetics Publishers
P.O. Box 80
Kingswood 5062
South Australia
374-0433

To our parents

Contents

Preface

Much of today's research and literature on athletes with eating disorders simply focuses on the number of individuals affected. We want to do more.

Coaches, team physicians, sport psychologists, athletic trainers, sport physical therapists, sport nutritionists, dance trainers, and other sport and medical professionals will find *Helping Athletes With Eating Disorders* a practical and comprehensive guide to effectively managing athletes with eating disorders.

Our goal is to provide you with practical recommendations to enhance the cooperative efforts of sport staff and medical personnel, while keeping foremost the special needs of the athlete with an eating disorder.

In addition to outlining formal treatment, *Helping Athletes With Eating Disorders* addresses daily management issues of helping athletes overcome their disorders. We examine the difficult subjects of eating, weighing, exercise and training, competition, medication, discipline, and personality difficulties. We address such topics as getting athletes into treatment, making referrals, handling injuries, ensuring privacy, and counseling the family.

Throughout the book, case examples are provided to explain and illustrate salient aspects of the difficulties facing athletes with eating disorders. The information contained in these cases accurately portrays athletes with eating disorders. However, in order to guard the privacy and confidentiality of the athletes involved, information that might identify particular individuals was changed. For this reason, case examples represent more of a typical case than a specific one.

We've organized the book into seven chapters. Chapter 1 outlines eating disorders from the clinical perspective, providing criteria for diagnosing anorexia nervosa, bulimia nervosa, and eating disorder not otherwise specified (NOS). Etiology and development are described along with related medical and psychological problems. Chapter 2 describes how sport participation can precipitate, maintain, and even exacerbate eating disorders.

Chapter 3 discusses sports that appear to place athletes at higher risk for developing eating problems. As we look at each sport, we describe the demands and expectations placed on these athletes as well as medical and other problems typical to these sports as they relate to low body weight or various eating-related behaviors.

Chapter 4 provides you with an in-depth look at the athlete with an eating disorder. Several case descriptions from different sports are presented. You will learn how these athletes view eating, exercise, sports, and injury. We list physical, psychological, and behavioral symptoms to help you identify athletes with eating disorders, and describe the effects of eating disorders on sport performance.

Chapters 5 and 6 present methods for managing eating disorders. You will learn when and how an athlete should be approached once an eating disorder is suspected, how to get the athlete into treatment, and how to handle issues such as resistance and confidentiality. We provide information on medication issues and guidelines to help you make important decisions about allowing further training and competition.

Chapter 7 focuses on preventive measures and strategies you can implement to reduce the risk that eating disorders will develop among athletes. We discuss the vital role of education in prevention and recommend how you can correct misinformation and influence attitudes and management styles that may contribute to the development or maintenance of eating disorders among some athletes.

What we hope we have presented in this book is a special management approach that will be viewed by athletes with eating disorders as sensitive and therapeutic. At the same time we hope you find it sensible and practical in meeting your goals and responsibilities as sport and treatment personnel.

Acknowledgments

Many people have played significant roles in our writing of this book—without their assistance its completion would certainly not have been possible. Although the role of our families and friends was somewhat indirect, their love, support, patience, and encouragement were of utmost importance and always appreciated. More directly, several individuals made significant and helpful comments after reading our early drafts. A special thank you goes to those who took the time to read and comment on the entire manuscript. Randall Dick, MS, and Michael Greenspan, PhD, saw promise in an early draft, and their recommendations greatly helped to organize and structure the book. Lionel Rosen, MD, and John Schrader, ATC, graciously volunteered their time and expertise in sport psychiatry and athletic training, respectively; their comments were most helpful. We offer a very special thank you to Steven J. (Jim) Sherman, PhD, who tirelessly read numerous drafts of the manuscript; we appreciate his contributions as critic, informal copyeditor, and cheerleader. We also thank the many people who talked with us about their sports: Indiana University coaches Sam Bell, Hobie Billingsley, Jeff Huber, Joe McFarland, Jill Sterkel, and Cheryl Ridall; Indiana University professors James Brown, Virginia Cesbron, Alice Lindeman, and John Raglin; University of Texas at Austin performance team director, Randa Ryan; former Olympian Jill Watson; and, most important, numerous athletes—whose names we will keep confidential—who are currently dealing with, or who have overcome, eating disorders and who were gracious, brave, and open enough to share this very personal facet of their lives with us. Finally, we thank the staff of Human Kinetics Publishers for their assistance in developing and producing this book. Special thanks to the publisher, Rainer Martens, who expressed interest in the topic of eating disorders among athletes, and to Mary Fowler, developmental editor, who worked with us throughout this project to enhance the final product.

Introduction

The athlete with an eating disorder is a member of a special population with a special problem. Unlike nonathletes with eating disorders, the athlete who has or is predisposed to have an eating disorder has difficulties which are complicated by a sport environment that may overemphasize performance, and also demand an ideal body size, shape, or weight. This ideal too often involves losing weight or body fat, which can precipitate an eating disorder in an athlete who is predisposed to develop an eating disorder or can exacerbate an existing disorder. Additionally, the sport environment may not only precipitate or worsen an eating disorder, it may also "legitimize" it.

With its emphasis on a lean body and through its endorsement of excessive exercise, the sport environment may make it easier for athletes to be eating disordered but more difficult for this disorder to be identified and subsequently treated. Additionally, many of the traits that are characteristic of individuals with eating disorders are also the characteristics found in good or elite athletes; individuals with an eating disorder and good (coachable) athletes both are usually compliant, willing to work hard (even to overwork themselves), perfectionistic, and able to withstand pain or discomfort, and they have a high need for achievement or superior performance. Thus, the expectations of the sport environment make it easy for the athlete with an eating disorder to hide within that environment and perhaps not receive necessary treatment.

Because the combination of eating disorders and sports makes for a special situation, the affected athlete requires special approaches to management and treatment. Unfortunately, a dearth of information is available in this area. Much of the research and literature that does exist has focused primarily on prevalence rates of anorexia nervosa and bulimia nervosa among athletes rather than on management of the disorder. Of course prevalence rates and related information are relevant and valuable to those individuals who work with athletes who have eating disorders. Nonetheless, the question of prevalence seems less important than the fact that too many athletes—regardless of how many and how this number compares to nonathletes—suffer from eating disorders and are in need of treatment.

The athlete with an eating disorder needs assistance from others. Currently, this assistance appears to be available from two very distinct and different sources or "worlds." The first is the sport world comprising coaches, athletic trainers, team physicians, and other sport personnel who are involved with the athlete on a day-to-day basis in the sport environment, as well as more specialized individuals such as sport psychologists and exercise physiologists. This group of individuals, which we refer to as the "sport management team," understands best the needs, expectations, demands, and pressures associated with training, competition, and sport performance, but the group members typically have little or no training in, or understanding of, eating disorders.

The second "world" or group that can assist the athlete with an eating disorder is made up of health care professionals trained and experienced in the diagnosis and treatment of eating disorders. These mental health professionals, physicians, and dietitians have a good understanding of the etiology and treatment of eating disorders. They are familiar with the emotional and cognitive aspects of these disorders and can provide appropriate therapeutic services. However, this group typically has little if any understanding of or experience with the sport environment.

The combination of eating disorders and sports presents a special situation. Each athlete who has an eating disorder is unique and requires special approaches to management and treatment. The most effective and efficient management and treatment of an athlete with an eating disorder lies within a cooperative effort of sport and treatment specialists. It is crucial for these individuals to determine how and when they can be most effective in helping an athlete overcome an eating disorder. The first step is recognizing the criteria necessary for the diagnosis of anorexia nervosa, bulimia nervosa, and eating disorder not otherwise specified (NOS). Chapter 1 provides such an overview and presents the medical and psychological problems associated with these disorders as well as their etiology and development.

Eating Disorders: The Clinical Condition

Eating disorders, which tend to result from an unhealthy combination of individual, sociocultural, familial, and biological factors, seriously threaten physical and psychological well-being. The most common are anorexia nervosa, bulimia nervosa, and one termed "eating disorder not otherwise specified" (NOS). In recent years, we have seen a burgeoning of reported eating disorders, in both the United States and other industrialized countries. But the nature of these disorders, as well as the way that prevalence data are collected and analyzed, make it difficult to determine just how widespread they are.

We know that for various reasons some individuals are more predisposed to develop eating disorders. Also, specific populations appear to be more at risk. Athletes constitute one such group, and subpopulations of athletes may face even greater risk. But before the interplay between sport and eating disorders can be fully understood and appreciated, we need to discuss the predisposing or etiological factors and clinical characteristics of eating disorders.

Demographic Issues

Eating disorders do not affect all segments of the population at the same rate. The three most influential demographic factors in the development of an eating disorder are gender, race, and age.

Gender

Numerous studies indicate that at least 90% of those with eating disorders are female. Why is this? Although eating disorders in males may be underreported, the disparity in large part is created by the different societal expectations for females and males, especially with respect to physical size, appearance, and attractiveness. Many people hold negative stereotypes about obesity and prejudice against women who are overweight, and media messages aimed at women promote the idea that beauty, success, personal worth, and happiness relate to being thin. Messages like these encourage women to do what it takes to be thin. Because of the traditional link created for women between physical appearance and personal worth, women who feel unattractive, unhappy, or unsuccessful often assume that they are not thin enough.

Some research suggests that males with eating disorders may tend to use excessive exercise rather than strict dieting or other pathogenic weight loss methods such as laxatives, diuretics, or diet pills. As a result, it may be more difficult for a male to recognize that he has an eating disorder. This, along with the denial that usually accompanies an eating disorder, makes it unlikely that the affected male will present himself for treatment. And even if he believes he has an eating problem, he may be reluctant to seek treatment for what he and many others consider a "woman's problem." Therefore, significantly more men may be eating disordered than we can presently identify from our current prevalence data. Also, as our society's emphasis on thinness is increasingly aimed at men, we can expect more men to diet. As more men diet, we can expect a concurrent increase in the prevalence of eating disorders in men. Nonetheless, most of our current knowledge about eating disorders is the result of research and treatment with females, and most individuals in treatment are female. For these reasons, we have used the feminine pronouns "she" and "her" often throughout this book.

Race

A person's race also has been found to be related to the development of eating disorders. Very low prevalence rates of anorexia nervosa and bulimia nervosa have been reported for blacks and other minority groups in the literature. Certainly, most individuals who present for treatment of eating disorders are white. This difference is probably due to the cultural expectations of various ethnic and racial groups. It has been suggested that blacks are less affected by sociocultural pressures to be thin.

What looks like a low incidence of eating disorders among nonwhites may be partly because minorities have not been systematically studied. Researchers have also suggested that socioeconomic factors may play a role in prevalence rates; it appears that nonwhites' risk of developing eating disorders increases as they embrace more of the middle- and upper-middle-class values of their white counterparts. We used to believe that eating disorders occurred only in higher socioeconomic classes; however, we now see individuals with eating disorders at all socioeconomic levels and may be seeing more nonwhite individuals with eating disorders in the future.

Age

Individuals with eating disorders are most often adolescents and young adults. The onset of these disorders usually occurs between ages 14 and 30, with anorexia often developing somewhat earlier than bulimia. Actually, eating disorders can occur at any age, but we rarely see young children or older adults with these disorders.

Anorexia Nervosa

Anorexia nervosa is often referred to as the self-starvation syndrome. It can occur at almost any stage of development but typically emerges first in early adolescence, often in response to the inevitable body changes that accompany puberty. Usually, the individual feels unhappy, unattractive, unworthy, and ineffectual. She believes that if she could be thinner, she would be happier. She begins to diet with what appears to be a "normal" desire to lose weight. Possibly, she really is overweight. Just as often, or perhaps more so, she only believes she is. As she diets and begins to lose weight, others comment on the change in her appearance. This gratifies her and encourages her to lose more. Perhaps for the first time in her life she sees herself as competent and even special because of her ability to lose weight.

As dieting and weight loss continue, weight loss becomes an important achievement while any lack of weight loss comes to be viewed as failure. The anorexic person begins to fear that the weight she has lost will return. To prevent this, she diets more stringently and may increase her exercise. As this process continues, she loses the ability to perceive her body accurately. As a result, she is apt to experience body-image distortion; that is, she sees herself as "fat" and needing to lose even more weight.

Obviously, as she becomes too thin and is eating very little, if at all, others begin to express their concern. The anorexic individual disregards it, maintaining that she is fine. From her perspective, she is not doing anything wrong. She is doing what many others in our society are doing—dieting. She believes she is simply doing a better job of it. Besides, she continues to see herself as needing to lose weight because she still has some "fat" that needs to be removed, or she needs to get into better shape. Additionally, she is reluctant to give up her newfound competence and sense of worth that has been established through her weight loss. Also, her weight loss may have finally gotten her the attention of a significant person in her life, and she fears losing that person's attention and concern if she regains her weight.

Etiology

Although the difficulties associated with puberty, as well as low self-esteem and unhappiness, play significant roles in the development of anorexia nervosa, not all individuals with these characteristics develop the disorder. Many complex, multidimensional factors influence the development and maintenance of the disorder in those who do become affected by it. Anorexia nervosa is really much more than dieting that has gone awry. Its primary purpose appears to be to provide a means through which the individual avoids dealing with difficult maturational or emotional issues.

In their classic text on anorexia nervosa, Garfinkel and Garner (1982) maintain that a combination of cultural, familial, and individual factors predispose an individual to the disorder. They view cultural pressures to be thin as a major contributing factor. The fact that this emphasis on thinness is aimed primarily at women explains in part why it is mostly women who develop the disorder. Garfinkel and Garner further believe that other sociocultural pressures on women such as increased expectations for high performance, achievement, and success increase the risk of developing anorexia nervosa.

In terms of familial factors, Garfinkel and Garner contend that probably no single family type is characteristic of anorexia nervosa. They do suggest, however, that families producing anorexic children often show a preoccupation with weight and eating; emphasize physical appearance; rely on external standards of measuring self-worth and success; report a history of affective disorder (depression) or alcoholism; and experience difficult parent-child interactions, especially as they relate to autonomy and separation.

Obviously, in our society not all families with these characteristics produce anorexic children. Familial characteristics and cultural pressures appear to set the stage for the disorder to develop; individual factors, however, then determine whether the disorder develops. Some of these factors Garfinkel and Garner identified include a need for approval (need to please); conformity (to maintain a sense of self-worth); conscientiousness; lack of responsiveness to inner needs; high personal expectations; all-or-nothing thinking; and concerns about autonomy, identity, and separation.

Along with the presence of predisposing factors, the process that leads to the disorder must be precipitated. Garfinkel and Garner, as well as most experts in the field, view dieting as the usual precipitant—dieting that is typically initiated by stressors in the individual's life, such as separation or loss, family problems, threats to self-esteem, environmental demands, or illness. Then once the anorexia process has begun, perpetuating factors maintain or sustain it, such as starvation effects; disturbance in body perception; and possible secondary rewards, including attention from significant others.

Diagnostic Criteria

The Diagnostic and Statistical Manual of Mental Disorders (Revised) (DSM-III-R; American Psychiatric Association, 1987) requires that for the diagnosis of anorexia nervosa to be made, an individual must refuse to maintain body weight over a minimal normal weight for height and age, have an intense fear of gaining weight or becoming fat even though he or she is underweight, have a distorted body image, and be amenorrheic if female.

Unfortunately, too much emphasis is often focused on the individual's weight in diagnosis (and treatment). What is important here is not a particular weight. An individual does not have to meet a particular weight criterion or even to be diagnosed as having anorexia nervosa to need treatment. Anorexia nervosa or a subclinical variant of it is like many other disorders in that recovery is often related to the chronicity of the disorder; if the disorder can be detected early, treatment is likely to proceed more quickly and easily and lead to a more positive outcome. Conversely, the longer a person has the disorder, the more entrenched she becomes in it. Anorexia nervosa typically increases in severity as duration increases and may become intractable.

DSM-III-R Diagnostic Criteria
for Anorexia Nervosa

1. Refusal to maintain body weight over a minimal normal weight for age and height, i.e., weight loss leading to maintenance of body weight 15% below that expected or failure to make expected weight gain during a period of growth, leading to body weight 15% below that expected
2. Intense fear of gaining weight or becoming fat, even though underweight
3. Disturbance in the way in which one's body weight, size, or shape is experienced, e.g., the person claims to "feel fat" even when emaciated or believes that one area of the body is "too fat," even when obviously underweight
4. In females, absence of at least three consecutive menstrual cycles when otherwise expected to occur (primary or secondary amenorrhea). (A woman is considered to have amenorrhea if her periods occur only following estrogen administration.)

From the *Diagnostic and Statistical Manual of Mental Disorders* (3rd ed., rev.) American Psychiatric Association, copyright 1987, p. 67. Reproduced with permission of the publisher.

The body image distortion characteristic of anorexia nervosa usually takes the form of the individual with anorexia seeing particular body parts or the entire body as fat. When she looks at her body, it appears larger than it actually is. She also expresses generally that she "feels fat." This fat feeling helps convince her that what she sees (fat) is what she is. There is some question as to whether body image distortion is perceptual or emotional in nature. However, the origin or explanation is of no consequence to the anorexic—she looks fat to herself and feels fat; therefore, she must *be* fat and as a consequence must lose weight to rectify this problem as quickly as possible.

Medical Characteristics and Problems

Anorexia nervosa can have quite debilitating and serious medical and physical consequences. Mitchell (1986) and Hsu (1990) provide in-depth discussions of the medical complications of anorexia. To summarize, amenorrhea is a common sign and symptom of anorexia nervosa. Other endocrine system problems might include abnormal estrogen metabolism, low testosterone levels, and abnormal thyroid function. Although amenorrhea is the hallmark of endocrine complications with anorexia nervosa, it may either directly or indirectly affect other systems, such as the skeletal system. It appears that amenorrhea may be related to bone mineral density loss and related complications such as osteoporosis and fractures (Drinkwater et al., 1984; Marcus et al., 1985; Shangold, Rebar, Wentz, & Schiff, 1990).

Gastric symptoms can involve every aspect of eating, from lack of appetite to vomiting (Waldholtz & Andersen, 1990). Typically, gastrointestinal complaints include pain, bloating, constipation, and postprandial distress (discomfort following eating). Another gastric complication may include delayed gastric emptying. Anorexics also may be at risk for pancreatic dysfunction in the form of pancreatitis.

In addition to hypotension and cardiac arrhythmias, cardiovascular complications often include bradycardia and decreased cardiac chamber dimensions. Electrocardiographic changes may occur as well as peripheral edema. Cardiac failure is a possibility during the refeeding phase of treatment as well as during the course of the illness. Hypothermia appears to be at least indirectly related to cardiac functioning. In the anorexic, it results from malnutrition and may affect cardiac functioning by decreasing heart rate, blood pressure, and cardiac output.

In most cases of anorexia nervosa, dehydration occurs as a result of fluid restriction, malnutrition, and purging in the form of induced vomiting or laxative or diuretic abuse. Electrolytes, which are necessary for healthy functioning of all the body's major systems, tend to be depleted through dehydration. Other problems associated with anorexia nervosa may include renal complications, hematological abnormalities, impaired respiratory function, and central nervous system complications. Metabolic abnormalities may include glucose homeostasis problems such as hypoglycemia. Liver function abnormalities may be present as well as elevated serum cholesterol levels.

Obviously, the most serious threat from anorexia nervosa is death. It is difficult to determine the mortality rate associated with the disorder. Studies have reported mortality rates from less than 1% to as high as 18%. This discrepancy may be accounted for in part by the length of time employed in follow-up studies. Typically, the longer the follow-up period, the more patients who died (Hsu, 1990). The most recent long-term study—a 10-year follow-up by Halmi (1991)—reported a mortality rate of 6.6%. Though mortality rates are primarily associated with women, it should not be assumed that only female anorexics die. Regardless of how mortality is measured, death usually results either directly or indirectly from emaciation or more specifically from cardiac failure or suicide.

For those individuals who survive anorexia nervosa, the lasting effects of the disorder vary with the medical complication as well as with the severity and chronicity of the disorder. Fortunately, as serious and dangerous as many of the aforementioned physical symptoms of anorexia are, most of them can be corrected through adequate nutrition and gradual weight restoration to more normal and healthy levels.

General Medical Signs and Symptoms of Anorexia Nervosa

1. Amenorrhea
2. Gastrointestinal problems
3. Cardiac arrhythmias
4. Hypotension
5. Hypothermia
6. Dehydration and electrolyte complications

Psychological and Behavioral Problems

It is often difficult to determine whether psychological problems cause anorexia or whether they result from the disorder. Nonetheless, if psychological problems precede the onset of anorexia, they are typically exacerbated by the disorder. These may include personality characteristics such as perfectionism, obsessionality, introversion, insecurity, rigidity of thinking, dependency, overcompliance, self-denial, and self-abasement (Strober, 1986). Emotional characteristics such as anxiety, fear, and depression, which often precede anorexia nervosa, also tend to worsen with the severity and chronicity of the disorder.

Psychological Characteristics or Effects of Anorexia Nervosa

1. Preoccupation with food
2. Irrational fear of being or becoming fat
3. Distorted body image
4. Significant body dissatisfaction
5. Low self-esteem
6. Depression, fear, anger, anxiety, and irritability

7. Difficulty expressing emotion in a direct manner
8. Perfectionism, obsessiveness, and high need for achievement
9. Absolute thinking
10. High need for approval (fear of disapproval)

Andersen (1986) suggested that other features such as difficulty concentrating, decreased emotional expressiveness, and food preoccupation, as well as social isolation and immature self-centeredness, generally result from the disorder and more specifically from starvation. Further, he suggested that the anorexic illness itself contributes to the symptoms of fear of fatness, the relentless pursuit of thinness, and body image distortion.

The question of what happens to these psychological problems once the patient has recovered is complex. Obviously, the issues that relate specifically to the illness itself will greatly decrease in the recovered patient; in fact, it is highly unlikely if not impossible for the individual to recover as long as these difficulties are operating. As might be expected, difficulties associated with starvation are also likely to be decreased or eliminated as a result of adequate nutrition and weight restoration, although it may take months beyond the restoration of weight for the body to fully recover.

Personality factors or characteristics associated with anorexia nervosa tend to be more resistant and are much less likely to change significantly after recovery. Any change tends to be minimal to moderate, with the personality characteristics perhaps becoming less disturbing or debilitating or in some cases more adaptive. However, even without a major personality change, a patient can often significantly alter many behaviors associated with these characteristics in healthier, more helpful ways. For example, the passive, dependent, and excessively compliant anorexic individual who always strives to please significant others at all costs may still have a strong need to please following recovery. Reasonable therapeutic changes might include her taking more control in her life, making more decisions based on what she really wants, and reducing the number of times she pleases others at her own expense.

What initially appear to be personality characteristics or even personality disorders in the anorexic patient are sometimes attenuated or even eliminated after she resumes normal eating patterns and weight levels. This suggests that attitudes and behaviors often attributed to personality factors may simply be a result of starvation.

Prevalence

Prevalence rates of anorexia nervosa have been equivocal due to several factors. First, anorexia is not readily discernible by the individual. Someone may be suffering from anorexia nervosa and not be aware of it. In fact, many anorexic individuals maintain that they have no problem. This factor coupled with the anorexic's fear of what treatment means—weight gain or becoming fat—makes it very difficult for the anorexic to present herself for treatment. Because most anorexic individuals are not likely to report having difficulty, much less present themselves for treatment, it is difficult to estimate the prevalence of the disorder. Second, methodological disparity in prevalence studies with regard to how data are collected and analyzed have probably influenced reported prevalence rates. Finally, as stated previously, special populations of individuals appear to have higher rates of anorexia nervosa and are at higher risk for the disorder because their activities or professions emphasize a particular size, shape, or weight—groups such as fashion models and ballet dancers. Although prevalence rates for groups like these may be quite high, the prevalence of anorexia nervosa in the general population appears to be less than 1%.

Bulimia Nervosa

The term bulimia nervosa has supplanted the older term bulimia in the recent revision of the DSM-III-R (American Psychiatric Association, 1987). This disorder has often been referred to in lay terms as the binge-purge syndrome.

A typical scenario for bulimia nervosa involves an individual who is unhappy and responds to an interaction of several predisposing factors with dieting, binge eating, and purging. As with anorexia, strong sociocultural pressures to be thin convince the unhappy or dissatisfied individual that her weight or body shape is the problem. Ironically, young women with bulimia tend to be attractive, high achieving, and very high functioning. Unfortunately, they are unable to perceive themselves as such.

The individual who will develop bulimia nervosa begins dieting in an effort to lose weight. For many of these individuals, the deprivation process of restrictive dieting leads to binge eating (Polivy & Herman, 1985). As hunger increases, the individual finds it more difficult to maintain tight control and restraint over eating because dieting leads to more thoughts of food. Attempts to move further below the body's set point weight (the genetically determined weight at which the body feels comfortable) increases appetite and slows down metabolism, making weight loss and weight maintenance more difficult. As this occurs, the individual becomes even more desperate about her weight and tries to diet even more stringently. At some point, she attempts to eat a small or reasonable amount of food but cannot maintain control. As she tries to reduce her control to allow for this eating, she finds moderation quite difficult, even impossible. In essence, she turns off her control and binges. Then, in an effort to undo the expected effects of binge eating (weight gain), she purges what she has eaten. Typically, this process involves induced vomiting but might additionally or alternatively involve laxative or diuretic abuse, excessive exercise, or fasting.

It also appears that as the individual is dieting, a psychological need to binge eat may occur. As the dieter deprives herself, she tends to create an even greater desire for the "forbidden" foods—actually inducing a psychological need to binge. In this way she is increasing the psychological value of eating and food.

Finally, binge eating and purging usually become a means through which the individual attempts to regulate or manage emotion. Bingeing and purging provide a distraction that at least momentarily allows the bulimic person to focus away from unpleasant or uncomfortable emotional concerns. The bulimic individual typically avoids open and direct expression of emotion for fear of displeasing significant others. As emotions are suppressed, tension and anxiety build. Some of this pent-up emotion is released through bingeing and purging.

Etiology

Researchers have proposed several explanations for the etiology of bulimia nervosa. Perhaps the most thorough is the "biopsychosocial" perspective of Johnson and Connors (1987). They suggest that the individual at risk for the disorder may have a biological vulnerability or predisposition to depression that "is exacerbated by both a family environment that is chaotic and conflictual and social role expectations that are confusing because they are in transition" (p. 149). The interaction of these factors leads to low self-esteem and problems with self-regulation. Society's emphasis on thinness helps the individual view weight loss as a solution to these problems. Unfortunately, however, dieting leads to binge eating, which in turn exacerbates low self-esteem and depression. In addition to alleviating the hunger associated with stringent dieting, binge eating also allows the individual to temporarily distract herself from difficult and unpleasant feelings. As a result, binge eating gradually becomes a strong and frequent response to emotionality in that the person with bulimia uses it to manage difficult and unpleasant feelings. However, the individual must then invoke purging behaviors—self-induced vomiting, laxative or diuretic abuse, fasting, or excessive exercise—to remove the guilt and shame associated with bingeing, as well as to avoid weight gain.

Obviously, most individuals with bulimia do not intend to engage in bingeing and purging on a frequent basis. Many typically begin by experimenting with purging, usually induced vomiting. However, each time these behaviors occur and provide relief, albeit temporary, they are strengthened. Unfortunately, they also lead to more shame, guilt, anger, and depression, which the individual with bulimia often manages through more bingeing and purging. Also, the individual is likely to believe that she must not eat as a consequence of her bingeing, and she decides to diet or fast. Deprivation associated with dieting leads to more binge eating, which in turn leads to purging. Finally, as the bingeing and purging continue, the individual comes to rationalize her behavior, finding more reasons for continuing it. As a result of these factors, what began as an infrequent, somewhat controlled experiment to manage eating and weight quickly becomes a compulsion that is out of the individual's control.

Sexual abuse can precede the onset of bulimia nervosa. Our inclusion of sexual abuse should not, however, be construed as a confirmation of its role as an etiological factor; its role is still unclear. This lack of clarity is in part related to the difficulty of knowing how many individuals with bulimia have experienced rape, incest, or molestation prior to the onset of the disorder; many of these abuse survivors are unable to remember their abuse experiences. Additionally, prevalence studies in this area may be further hampered by a lack of methodological consistency. Consequently, estimates of sexual abuse among individuals with bulimia have varied from 7% (Lacey, 1990) to 64% (Oppenheimer, Howells, Palmer, & Chaloner, 1985). Regardless of how high reported rates are, they are meaningful only from an etiological standpoint when compared to base rates among women in the general population or in other psychiatric groups. Accurate and consistent data in this area are still being collected.

We do know that for those individuals with bulimia who have experienced sexual abuse, many of the issues and problems characteristic of bulimia nervosa—feeling out of control, body dissatisfaction, low self-esteem, and depression—may be related at least in part to that abuse. Sometimes during treatment for bulimia nervosa, an individual will recall or deal with her abuse experiences for the first time, and it can be crucial to the individual's recovery.

Diagnostic Criteria

The DSM-III-R (American Psychiatric Association, 1987) criteria for bulimia nervosa include recurrent episodes of binge eating, a feeling of a lack of control over eating behavior during binges, purging that might include self-induced vomiting or laxative or diuretic use, strict dieting or fasting, vigorous exercise to prevent weight gain, and persistent overconcern with body shape and weight.

Binge eating, though described as the rapid consumption of a large amount of food in a discrete period of time, can be quite variable. What constitutes "a large amount" will vary, as will "a discrete period of time." The individual with bulimia employs different criteria in describing or evaluating her bingeing. A binge may mean ingesting a large number of calories (e.g., 5,000) during one eating experience or episode. Or it may involve eating thousands of calories during an entire day, which might be considered one all-day binge or two or three smaller binges. The individual may also define bingeing by the type of food eaten. For one male marathoner, binge foods were high-calorie sweets. A binge for him frequently included at least a dozen doughnuts and a half-gallon of ice cream. For another individual, a binge may involve eating a small amount of a sweet food or another food that she considers "bad"—that is, a food that she does not view as an acceptable part of her normal regimen. Although most binge-eating episodes probably involve the ingestion of at least some sweet foods, almost any food such as cereal or crackers can serve as a binge food or trigger binge eating if the individual's nutritional and psychological state places him or her at risk.

Probably more important than the amount or type of food the individual eats is why the food is eaten, how the person feels as a consequence, and how the eating is compensated for. As mentioned previously, the individual with bulimia may be bingeing for several reasons—as a result of dieting, or in an effort to manage unpleasant emotion.

DSM-III-R Diagnostic Criteria for Bulimia Nervosa

1. Recurrent episodes of binge eating (rapid consumption of a large amount of food in a discrete period of time)
2. A feeling of lack of control over eating behavior during the eating binges
3. Regularly engaging in self-induced vomiting, the use of laxatives or diuretics, strict dieting or fasting, or vigorous exercise in order to prevent weight gain
4. A minimum of two binge-eating episodes a week for at least three months
5. Persistent overconcern with body shape and weight

From the *Diagnostic and Statistical Manual of Mental Disorders* (3rd ed., rev.) American Psychiatric Association, copyright 1987, pp. 68-69. Reproduced with permission of the publisher.

Purging not only relieves the physical discomfort associated with gastric dilatation, it also temporarily alleviates some of the emotional discomfort. Unfortunately, each time the individual purges, bingeing is legitimized—by undoing the binge, purging makes bingeing more likely to occur in the future.

Medical Characteristics and Problems

Bulimia nervosa differs from anorexia nervosa in that medical complications result from different sources. Whereas most complications of anorexia nervosa occur as a direct or indirect result of starvation, complications of bulimia nervosa occur as a result of bulimic behaviors—most notably binge eating and purging. Hsu (1990), Johnson and Connors (1987), and Mitchell (1990) provide excellent information on the medical problems encountered by many individuals with bulimia. Problems and complications of bulimia nervosa can be found in all the body's major systems. Endocrine system problems often involve disturbance of menses. Some bulimics may exhibit amenorrhea, whereas others may show menstrual irregularity. Although true amenorrhea characteristic of the anorexic is much rarer in the bulimic, menstrual irregularities are common and can occur even when the individual's weight is within a normal range.

Dental problems and gum disease occur frequently in the bulimic who is vomiting. Erosion of tooth enamel and increased cavities are common due to the gastric acid that is in the mouth from vomiting.

As would be expected, gastrointestinal complications can be numerous. These include simple and frequent problems such as swollen parotid glands, abdominal cramps, bloating, constipation, and diarrhea. More serious and less frequently occurring gastric problems include loss of the gag reflex, esophagus-related difficulties such as esophagitis and ulceration or perforation, and stomach-related difficulties such as slowed gastric emptying, spontaneous or reflex regurgitation, gastric and duodenal ulcers, and even stomach rupture. Laxative abuse may lead to loss of normal bowel function with consequent constipation and bleeding.

Electrolyte abnormalities and dehydration appear to be frequent complications of purging. Typically, electrolytes such as potassium, sodium, and chloride are lost as a result of dehydration. Electrolyte balance is necessary for proper functioning of the body's major systems—most notably, the cardiovascular system. Cardiovascular complications often include dehydration with associated water retention and edema, as well as hypotension with dizziness, light-headedness, and fainting. Cardiomyopathy may develop as a result of the abuse of ipecac, a popular emetic many bulimics use to induce vomiting.

Medical Signs and Symptoms of Bulimia Nervosa

1. Menstrual irregularities
2. Dental and gum disease
3. Swollen parotid glands
4. Gastrointestinal problems
5. Electrolyte abnormalities and dehydration

Fortunately, with the exception of dental erosion, many of these medical problems can be corrected and reversed once an individual has ended the bulimic behaviors and implemented a more normal eating regimen. Even though most medical problems characteristic of bulimia nervosa are reversible, this should in no way be construed to mean that these problems are not serious and debilitating.

Psychological Problems

As with anorexia nervosa, many psychological problems precede or help produce bulimia nervosa, whereas others may be a result of, or may be exacerbated by, the disorder. Some of these are quite similar to those characteristic of the anorexic, such as those that relate specifically to eating, low emotional expressiveness, and a high need for approval. Also, low self-esteem, low tolerance for frustration and anxiety, and affective instability (depression, anger, anxiety) typically play a role in the development of bulimia nervosa. These characteristics have been described in other sources (e.g., Johnson & Connors, 1987; Sherman & Thompson, 1990) and will not be recounted here. Suffice it to say that they describe individuals who neither like nor feel good about themselves, have difficulty waiting for what they want, and show variability of mood or mood swings that are often related to depression.

Psychological Characteristics or Effects of Bulimia Nervosa

1. Preoccupation with food
2. Relentless pursuit of thinness
3. Unusual eating habits and behaviors
4. Low self-esteem
5. Impulsivity or low sense of self-control
6. Affective instability (depression, anger, anxiety)
7. Difficulty expressing emotion in a direct manner
8. Low frustration tolerance
9. Absolute thinking
10. Significant body dissatisfaction
11. High need for approval (fear of disapproval)

Although these characteristics may play a role in the development of bulimia nervosa, they often help maintain the disorder as well. At the same time, they may be exacerbated as the severity and chronicity of the disorder increase. More specifically, bulimic individuals will likely feel worse about themselves, display less impulse control, become more depressed, and exhibit a decline in social functioning. As these problems or characteristics worsen, the individual's need to binge and purge increases in her effort to manage the difficult feelings they engender. Of course, as bulimic symptoms increase, the individual feels even worse, which perpetuates the cycle.

Behavioral Problems

Related to the psychological characteristics and problems associated with bulimia nervosa are several problem behaviors. Many individuals with bulimia have difficulties with alcohol and other drugs. Substance abuse in bulimics may be related to the individual's indirect approach to managing emotions in general and depression in particular. Perhaps abuse problems arise from the bulimic individual's low frustration tolerance and need for immediate gratification. Substance abuse problems may also be related to the relatively high prevalence of alcoholism in family members of bulimic individuals.

In a subset of people with bulimia nervosa, problems involving impulse control may include stealing and self-destructive behavior. A bulimic who steals often takes items directly related to the bulimic symptom complex, such as food or laxatives. In terms of self-destructive behavior, a subgroup of bulimics periodically engage in self-abuse or mutilation or make suicidal gestures or attempts. Self-destructive behaviors are probably related to a combination of factors that include poor impulse control, depression, substance abuse, and personality traits.

Prevalence

As with anorexia nervosa, prevalence rates for bulimia nervosa reported in the literature have been equivocal for several reasons. First, the secrecy associated with the disorder makes prevalence estimation difficult. Second, much of the data in prevalence studies have come as a result of questionnaire research. The difficulties involved with this type of self-report data have been recounted numerous times (Hsu, 1990; Johnson & Connors, 1987; Mitchell & Eckert, 1987). Third, earlier studies used the less stringent criteria for bulimia, whereas more recent studies have employed the more stringent and specific criteria for bulimia nervosa. Obviously, the more stringent the criteria necessary for the diagnosis, the lower the prevalence rate. As with anorexia nervosa, special populations, such as female college students, appear to have higher prevalence rates of bulimia nervosa. However, the prevalence of the disorder in the general population is probably between 1% and 5%.

Eating Disorder Not Otherwise Specified (NOS)

The diagnosis of an eating disorder is not as straightforward as it may sound. The diagnostic criteria make it seem as though an individual either meets the criteria for anorexia nervosa or bulimia nervosa or is not considered eating disordered. However, eating disorders tend to occur on a continuum—that is, some eating disorders may be difficult to distinguish because the individual may not meet all criteria for a particular disorder. For example, an individual may meet all criteria for anorexia nervosa except amenorrhea, or she may not be 15% below normal body weight. If an individual meets all criteria for anorexia nervosa but also binges and purges, what is the correct diagnosis? What if the person meets all criteria for bulimia nervosa but is more than 15% below normal body weight? The diagnostic category of "eating disorder not otherwise specified" or "eating disorder NOS" is used to cover patients who do not meet all criteria for either anorexia nervosa or bulimia nervosa (American Psychiatric Association, 1987). Although it might be convenient for individuals to fit neatly into categories, in reality many individuals have idiosyncratic eating disturbances. The diagnostic category of eating disorder NOS acknowledges the existence and importance of a variety of eating disturbances.

It bears repeating that eating disorders occur on a continuum; some individuals with anorexia may exhibit behaviors characteristic of bulimia, such as purging but without bingeing. Many individuals with bulimia would like to be able to not eat consistently, and in an effort to control bingeing and purging, they try to restrict their intake much as anorexics do. Their restrictive dieting, however, leads to binge eating. Many individuals with bulimia nervosa have previously been anorexic. Some individuals alternate between the two disorders. Actually, more individuals may meet the diagnostic criteria for eating disorder NOS than for the more specific and restrictive criteria of anorexia or of bulimia nervosa.

A functional and practical rather than descriptive approach to diagnosis suggests that the primary issue here is not whether an individual meets all the specific criteria for anorexia nervosa or bulimia nervosa. Rather, one of the primary issues involves the extent to which the individual's physical and emotional well-being is being compromised as a result of eating-related symptoms and to what extent these symptoms interfere with adequate functioning in everyday life.

DSM-III-R Diagnostic Criteria for Eating Disorder NOS

Disorders of eating that do not meet the criteria for a specific Eating Disorder.

Examples:

1. A person of average weight does not have binge-eating episodes, but frequently engages in self-induced vomiting in fear of gaining weight
2. All of the features of Anorexia Nervosa in a female except absence of menses
3. All of the features of Bulimia Nervosa except the frequency of binge-eating episodes

From the *Diagnostic and Statistical Manual of Mental Disorders* (3rd ed., rev.) American Psychiatric Association, copyright 1987, p. 71. Reproduced with permission of the publisher.

A second critical issue relates to treatment. As mentioned previously, an individual with disturbed eating does not have to meet all diagnostic criteria before treatment is warranted. In fact, individuals with subclinical variants of anorexia nervosa and bulimia nervosa—that is, whose eating disturbances have fewer, less severe, and less chronic symptoms—tend to be easier to treat than those who have developed the full clinical disorder. Although our current knowledge and understanding of subclinical cases are limited due to a dearth of research in the area, these cases nonetheless are important for several reasons. First, we can probably assume that many cases of anorexia or bulimia nervosa begin as subclinical variants of these disorders, and early identification and treatment may prevent development of the full disorder. Further, subclinical cases probably outnumber cases of disorders that meet diagnostic criteria.

Obesity and Compulsive Overeating

Although obesity may be a medical problem for some individuals resulting from a variety of factors that might include dysfunctional eating, it is not currently considered an eating *disorder* as classified in professional diagnostic manuals. Additionally, many individuals report difficulty with "compulsive overeating," but this too is not currently listed in the DSM-III-R as an eating disorder. For this reason, we will not include discussions of obesity and compulsive overeating in this book. A final note in this regard involves the next proposed revision of the DSM, which should be available in 1993 or 1994. In addition to possible alterations in the diagnostic criteria for anorexia nervosa, bulimia nervosa, and eating disorder NOS, DSM-IV may contain a new diagnostic category called "binge-eating disorder," which may be relevant for some obese individuals as well as for many compulsive overeaters.

CHAPTER 2

The Impact of Sport

To understand the interplay between eating disorders and athletes, we must examine the various aspects of the sport environment that can contribute to the development and maintenance of eating disorders. To do this, we first need to determine the scope of the problem. In this regard, we will discuss the prevalence rates of eating disorders in athletes and the factors that appear to affect those rates. We will then discuss the role sport can play in precipitating and maintaining an eating disorder. Relatedly, we will examine attitudes and practices in the sport world regarding ideal body weight, body fat, and performance that may place athletes at risk for developing disorders. Finally, working from the notion that athletes constitute a special population, we will discuss diagnostic issues that warrant special consideration in the identification of athletes who need treatment.

Prevalence

Eating disorders may be more of a problem for some athletes than for the general population. In addition to facing the same factors that place nonathletes at risk for developing eating disorders, athletes appear to be at increased risk due to factors within the sport environment. More specifically, segments of the sport community have in recent years strongly emphasized the relationship between low body fat composition and enhanced athletic performance. As a result, many athletes are being asked to lose weight so they can perform or compete better. Unfortunately, the athletes usually pursue this weight loss through dieting—the primary precursor to the development of an eating disorder.

Also, within this special population, smaller subpopulations of athletes may be at even greater risk for developing eating disorders. Many of the traits that are characteristic of individuals with eating disorders are also the traits found in good or elite athletes. Both individuals with eating disorders and good (coachable) athletes are usually compliant, are willing to work hard (even to overwork), are perfectionistic, have a high need for achievement or superior performance, and are able to withstand pain or discomfort.

Prevalence rates for eating disorders in athletes have been equivocal. Some studies have reported a high incidence (Burckes-Miller & Black, 1988; Clark, Nelson, & Evans, 1988; Gadpaille, Sanborn, & Wagner, 1987). Others, however, have found a low incidence (Selby, Weinstein, & Bird, 1990; Sherman & Thompson, 1991; Weight & Noakes, 1987) that appears to be comparable to the rates typically found in the general population. Rather than looking at the prevalence of anorexia nervosa and bulimia nervosa per se, some researchers have investigated behaviors and attitudes characteristic of those disorders. Here too, results have been equivocal. A series of studies by Rosen and associates (Dummer, Rosen, Heusner, Roberts, & Counsilman, 1987; Rosen & Hough, 1988; Rosen, McKeag, Hough, & Curley, 1986) found that athletes frequently exhibited pathogenic behaviors and attitudes associated with eating or weight. When comparing levels of eating disturbance in athletes to those in nonathletes, however, Pasman and Thompson (1988) found minimal or no differences, and Wilkins, Boland, and Albinson (1991) found lower levels of pathological eating behaviors and attitudes in their athlete sample. Relatedly, Owens and Slade (1987) reported only minimal similarities between athletes and eating disorder patients.

Apparently, several factors play a role in the equivocal nature of results reported in these prevalence studies. Just as in studies of the general population, the most important of these appears to involve methodology, especially how prevalence data are collected and analyzed. In many prevalence studies athletes were asked to complete questionnaires to determine if they met diagnostic criteria for an eating disorder. The potential risks and unreliability of such a procedure have been discussed frequently (e.g., Hsu, 1990; Johnson & Connors, 1987; Mitchell & Eckert, 1987). A second factor, special populations, is probably more important in explaining equivocal prevalence rates and therefore will be our major focus in this section. As we mentioned previously, athletes seem to constitute a special population with regard to eating disorders, and subpopulations within it appear to be at a greater or lesser risk of developing an eating disorder. If this is the case, these subpopulations may be affecting or biasing the prevalence data for the entire athletic population because they are represented differently in different studies. The subpopulations in question consist of (1) athletes in what we refer to as "thinness-demand" sports and (2) black athletes.

Thinness-Demand Sports

Researchers have suggested that activities that emphasize or require a small body size, thin shape, or low weight tend to increase the likelihood or prevalence of eating disorders in participating subjects (Garfinkel & Garner, 1982; Shisslak, Crago, Neal, & Swain, 1987). Consequently, athletes in "thinness-demand" activities— sports that for a variety of reasons encourage thinness—would be expected to show a higher rate of eating disorders. More specifically, athletes in the so-called "appearance" sports such as gymnastics, diving, and figure skating, which focus on form in their scoring, would be expected to be at higher risk for developing eating disorders. Individuals involved in activities such as distance running and ballet, which emphasize a very thin, lean body, would also appear to be at higher risk. Although the research in this area is inconclusive, some studies have found greater tendencies toward eating disorders in athletes from thinness-demand sports (Borgen & Corbin, 1987; Davis & Cowles, 1989). These findings raise an interesting question: If thinness-demand athletes were eliminated from prevalence studies, how would prevalence rates for the general athlete population be affected? Would athletes then show a rate of eating disorders lower than or similar to that of nonathletes? If so, this would suggest that the key issue is one of thinness rather than simply sport participation.

Impact of Race

Whereas demand for thinness seems to play a direct role in the prevalence of eating disorders in athletes, the role or impact of an athlete's race on eating disorder prevalence appears to be less direct but more complex. As mentioned in chapter 1, the prevalence of eating disorders among nonwhites is quite low. With athletes, the variable of race relates specifically to black athletes—the largest nonwhite athlete group in the United States. The fact that black women are significantly less likely than Caucasian women to develop anorexia nervosa or bulimia nervosa has been discussed numerous times (Andersen & Hay, 1985; Garfinkel & Garner, 1982; Gray, Ford, & Kelly, 1987; Hsu, 1987). Despite this fact, there is a dearth of literature investigating the relationship between the race of athletes and the prevalence of eating disturbance.

Based on the low incidence of eating disorders among blacks in the general population, we would expect a similarly low incidence among black athletes. Although this is an interesting supposition in itself, the relationship between the black athlete and eating disturbance may be more complex, involving not only the variable of race but also the possibility that white and black athletes are differentially represented in thinness-demand sports. This differential representation in particular sports may have confounded prevalence studies with athletes. Specifically, the higher risk thinness-demand sports—distance running, diving, figure skating, and gymnastics—are typically sports in which black athletes are underrepresented. This suggests that the low number of black athletes in the higher risk sports, or the higher number of blacks in the sports that appear to pose a low risk for eating disorders (i.e., basketball, softball, volleyball, etc.), may be biasing prevalence rates in studies of athletes. Our research (Sherman & Thompson, 1991) lends support to this notion; we found a trend indicating an inverse relationship between percentage of black athletes on a collegiate women's team and the mean number of eating disorder risk indicators for each athlete on that team. Most important, however, was that the highest percentages of black athletes—56.3% and 54.5%—were found in the non-thinness demand sports of sprinting and basketball, respectively. Conversely, only 7.7% of the athletes in all the thinness-demand activities were black. A similar trend was reported in a survey of NCAA member institutions (NCAA, 1988). The NCAA found that basketball and track had the highest percentages of black women athletes in all NCAA divisions, with 21.9% and 19.7%, respectively. At the same time, low percentages of black women were found in thinness-demand sports such as gymnastics (2.2%) and cross-country (6.3%). The report stated that blacks are almost nonexistent in some sports such as swimming (0.4%). It is interesting to note that the essentially white sport of swimming appears to have a relatively high incidence of eating disorders among participants.

Sport and Eating Disorders

Participation in athletics is apparently related to the development of eating disorders in some athletes. However, the exact nature of that relationship has yet to be fully determined. The possibilities that we believe are the most likely and relevant are as follows:

1. Aspects of sport or of specific sports *attract* individuals who are either eating disordered or who are at risk for the development of an eating disorder.
2. Participation in sport or in specific sports *causes* eating disorders.
3. Sport or participation in some sports does not cause the disorder but *precipitates* its development in athletes who are *predisposed* to have a disorder.

Attraction to Sport

Because sports that emphasize thinness apparently show higher prevalence rates of eating disorders among participants than those without that emphasis, we can assume that thinness demand plays a role in the relationship between sport and eating disorders. One explanation for this is that thinness-demand sports attract individuals who are either eating disordered or at risk for developing an eating disorder. In this regard, Sacks (1990) has suggested that many anorexic individuals are attracted to sports like distance running and gymnastics that hide their illness. This seems to imply that the individual is already anorexic, at least in attitude if not in behavior or weight, before participating in sport.

This attraction to particular sports is probably in part related to the emphasis on, and legitimization of, thinness in those sports. In other words, the demands or requirements for thinness or smallness in these sports make it easier for the athlete to "hide," as Sacks suggests. As a society and within the sport community, we have become conditioned to expect certain athletes to have a particular size or shape. For example, football players are huge and basketball players are tall, whereas jockeys are short, distance runners are expected to be thin, and female gymnasts are supposed to be tiny. These stereotyped standards make it difficult for observers to notice when a particular athlete has moved too far in the expected direction in terms of size, shape, or weight. It can be difficult to see a gymnast as too small or a distance runner as too thin. Conversely, however, it is much easier to notice a large gymnast or heavy distance runner.

The exercise component of a particular sport may also attract an at-risk individual. Endurance sports or activities that require endurance training are apt to be attractive to someone who overvalues exercise or who uses excessive exercise as a means of weight loss or purgation. Outside the sport environment, others may criticize an individual for spending too much time exercising, saying that it takes up too much time or interferes with more important aspects of his or her life. This same person is much less likely to be criticized in a sport environment that either implicitly or explicitly communicates the necessity of excessive levels of exercise, and even rewards it. If this person is noticed in the sport environment, it may be because he or she is viewed as a very hard-working athlete who is deeply committed to becoming better.

Unfortunately, these common and accepted weight and exercise standards in many sports that help athletes hide their disorder make it more difficult for people around the athlete to identify a problem, and also make it more difficult for athletes themselves to see the need for intervention. This might delay the treatment of an affected athlete, allowing an eating disorder to go undetected until the athlete's physical health and emotional well-being have been significantly or even dangerously compromised.

The attraction to sport hypothesis appears to have merit in that it can at least in part explain why some at-risk individuals are attracted to thinness-demand and endurance sports and how these sports may increase the risk for these athletes. On the other hand, it does not adequately explain how an elite gymnast, for example, who was selected at age 5 to begin intensive, high-level training develops an eating disorder 10 years later. Obviously, we cannot say that she was attracted to gymnastics at such a young age because she overvalued thinness or exercise. The attraction hypothesis also does not adequately explain the presence of eating disorders in sports that do not demand thinness or endurance training.

Causation

The notion that participation in sport causes eating disorders in athletes can probably be attributed to two factors. The first is that high levels of physical activity or exercise can cause an eating disorder to develop. The second involves the pressures or demands for thinness inherent in particular sports or emphasized by particular coaches.

Activity-Induced Anorexia.   Credence for the notion that sports may induce or cause anorexia nervosa comes from hypotheses suggesting that high levels of physical activity or exercise can lead to the development of an eating disorder. Such a biobehavioral model of activity-based anorexia nervosa was proposed in a series of studies by Epling, Pierce, and their associates (Epling & Pierce, 1984, 1988; Epling, Pierce, & Stefan, 1981, 1983; Pierce, Epling, & Boer, 1986). They suggest that dieting and exercise initiate the anorexic cycle. Specifically, they contend that strenuous exercise tends to suppress appetite, which serves to decrease the value of food reinforcement. As a result, food intake decreases and body weight is lost. As body weight decreases, the motivational value of activity (exercise) increases. This leads to an increase in physical exercise, which in turn decreases the value of eating. Epling and Pierce believe that this cycle maintains itself once it is initiated. More specifically with regard to anorexia nervosa, they suggest that these high levels of exercise may significantly reduce food intake in some individuals to the point that anorexia develops. Epling and his colleagues have suggested that as many as 75% of the cases of anorexia are activity- or exercise-induced.

As plausible as the activity-based explanation for anorexia nervosa sounds, some conditions it cannot explain. For example, not all anorexic individuals exercise. Also, the activity-based hypothesis places exercise as the central point in the anorexic process. For some anorexic individuals who exercise, their exercise does not appear to be the crucial element in the process that leads to anorexia. Relatedly, in this explanation exercise exerts its effects from the beginning of the process. Of the anorexics who exercise, many begin exercising only after caloric restriction and weight loss have taken place. Finally, the activity-based explanation does not explain bulimia nervosa.

Pressures to Lose Weight.   As we discussed in chapter 1, dieting is the primary precursor to the development of an eating disorder. Encouragement or demand for reduced weight or body fat has become quite popular in sport circles today. Many athletes, depending on their sport, feel the pressure inherent in their sport to diet to reduce weight and body fat in an effort to enhance athletic performance. They may also feel pressure from their coaches to lose weight, and it is important not to underestimate the power many coaches have with their athletes. Athletes often indicate that they diet because their coaches encouraged or told them to do so. As an example, a study by Rosen and Hough (1988) with collegiate gymnasts indicated that 67% of the gymnasts they surveyed had been told by their coaches that they were too heavy. The fact that 75% of the gymnasts in Rosen and Hough's study used pathogenic weight control methods indicates that some athletes are willing to do whatever it takes to please their coaches in this regard. Because dieting is easily encouraged and reinforced by many aspects of the sport environment, including powerful coaches, it is easy to believe as some do that these pressures to diet are causing eating disorders in athletes.

Athletic Participation as Precipitant

We know that in some athletes dieting leads to the development of an eating disorder. Relatedly, sports that emphasize thinness apparently show higher prevalence rates of eating disorders than those without that emphasis. Thus, we can assume that thinness demand plays a role in the development of eating disorders. However, for reasons discussed earlier, the relationship between aspects of the sport environment that encourage or demand dieting or thinness do not appear to directly cause eating disorders to develop. This should be apparent from an examination of eating disorders in the nonsport world. Of course, not all nonathletes who diet or exercise develop an eating disorder. And not all individuals in nonsport activities that demand thinness develop an eating disorder. Modeling provides an excellent example. Although there is a high incidence of eating disorders among professional models, obviously not all models have them. Thus, it seems plausible to assume that the same process that operates in the nonsport world also operates within the sport world: An individual who is predisposed to develop a disorder places him- or herself at higher risk by dieting. By "predisposed," we mean the interaction of the individual, sociocultural, familial, and biological factors discussed in chapter 1 that place a person at risk for developing an eating disorder.

Although sport participation does not directly cause eating disorders, it may precipitate a disorder in an at-risk athlete through its emphasis on the relationship between a thin or small shape and enhanced sport performance. For example, a coach may require or strongly recommend low weight levels for his or her athletes. This is apt to make many if not all of the athletes diet. And it may subsequently precipitate eating-disordered behavior in some of the athletes. It is unlikely, however, to precipitate a disorder in all of them. Some of the athletes will ignore the coach's demands or be unperturbed by them. Some will be able to comply with these demands without developing disorder symptoms. Others may quit the team. These athletes are less *predisposed* to develop an eating disorder. If an athlete is predisposed to develop an eating disorder, then pressures to diet and please a coach can serve as a catalyst for the process to begin.

With regard to predisposing factors, Johnson and Connors (1987) attempted to explain how the pursuit of thinness by the person with bulimia relates to individual or personality factors. Two of these factors—self-regulatory deficits and achievement expectations—appear to be particularly relevant to the athlete with bulimia. Johnson and Connors suggested that self-regulatory deficits involve a need to be in control of one's body in particular and one's life in general. Through mastery of the body—that is, through becoming thinner or by reducing body fat—the individual can feel more in control. This appears to be related to the athlete with bulimia in several ways. First, being proficient at a sport allows the individual another avenue for mastery or control of the body. Second, the physical training demanded by most sports provides the person with another means by which to lose weight or reduce body fat. Third, the emphasis on leanness and its purported positive relationship with sport performance legitimize the athlete's relentless pursuit of thinness.

In terms of achievement expectations, Johnson and Connors view the bulimic individual as having few socially valued means by which to compete and achieve. They suggest that the pursuit of thinness provides such a means, given the value our society has assigned to thinness. With their emphasis on thinness, many sports could give the individual another activity option consistent with the pursuit of thinness. Additionally, with the value that much of our society currently places on sports and athletes, this environment provides an individual with a socially valued arena in which to compete and achieve.

We have just described how two predisposing personality characteristics can play a role in an athlete's bulimia. However, other individual, familial, social, or biological factors may play similar roles. It is important to remember that an athlete is unlikely to develop an eating disorder without the necessary predisposing factors. And this would be true even for an athlete in a thinness-demand sport whose coach required a suboptimal weight. However, this should in no way be construed to mean that coaches who demand thinness do not play a role in the development of an eating disorder. They most assuredly can and do. Also, these demanding coaches may have more athletes with disorders than their less demanding counterparts. Nonetheless, even though coaches can increase the risk of eating disorder development and can indirectly precipitate a disorder by exerting pressure to lose weight, they do not necessarily create or cause eating disorders. The case of one gymnast is illustrative.

CASE STUDY

Jennifer

When Jennifer sought treatment for her bulimia nervosa at age 20, she had had her disorder for 6 years. Her history indicated that emotion was not expressed openly in her family, other than her father's occasional angry outbursts. She reported that his anger—his only show of emotion—scared her. Jennifer feared that she did not please him and was very much concerned with seeking his approval and acceptance. She reported that her symptoms began when her gymnastics coach suggested she lose 10 pounds in an effort to perform better. Up to that point (age 14), she had enjoyed gymnastics. She had recently gained weight as a result of going through puberty. She was not particularly happy about her body, but neither had she thought much about losing weight. She wanted to please her coach and was more than willing to try to lose weight. Her very restrictive dieting led to binge eating, which in turn led to self-induced vomiting. She was able to lose only a minimal amount of weight through her bulimia and was unable to detect a change in her athletic performance. Jennifer was frustrated by her coach being more attentive to and "playing favorites" with the girls who performed better. She had also noticed that these girls were usually the thinnest on her team. Due to her frustration with not being "thin enough" and not being able to lose weight, Jennifer eventually gave up gymnastics before completing her high school eligibility. Unfortunately, however, she was not able to give up her bulimia.

Jennifer's story clearly indicates the power of a coach in recommending weight loss. It also indicates that Jennifer's dieting in an effort to please him precipitated her bulimic behaviors. But did he cause the disorder to develop? If the coach was the primary causative agent in this process, we would expect most or all of his gymnasts to become eating disordered. Jennifer was unaware of whether eating disorders developed in any of her teammates who were also encouraged to diet. It appears that Jennifer's upbringing in an emotionally nonexpressive family and her need to please significant others in her life—most notably her father—had probably predisposed her to develop her disorder. She was also going through puberty at the time and attempting to deal with the typical bodily and psychological changes that occur at that stage of development. Her coach encouraged her to lose weight (diet). Her dieting then precipitated her symptoms. For these reasons, we can therefore conclude that neither her coach nor her participation in gymnastics caused her disorder. We can conclude, however, that some of her teammates could have developed the disorder if they had been predisposed to do so and had responded with dieting.

We noted earlier that sports such as gymnastics and distance running with higher prevalence rates of eating disorders may attract more individuals who are predisposed to those disorders. And, as discussed previously, this attraction is probably related in part to the emphasis on, and legitimization of, thinness, or exercise in these sports. In essence, some athletes bring their disorders, or at least the predisposition to their disorders, to their sports. In these cases, a sport can either precipitate a disorder or help *maintain* an existing disorder. This is demonstrated in the case of Laura.

CASE STUDY

Laura

Laura had grown up in a very traditional family in which problems had not been dealt with directly. As a result, she believed that no one wanted to deal with her problems or her feelings about them, and that she had to deal with them herself if they were to be resolved. Perhaps more important, Laura did not want to displease anyone by talking about how depressed she felt or impose on them by asking for what she wanted or needed. Unfortunately, her lack of experience in problem management and her low self-esteem made dealing directly with her problems improbable if not impossible. Despite being quite attractive and perfectionistic regarding her appearance, Laura saw herself as "fat and ugly." She was convinced that she would be much happier if she could only be thinner. Before age 18, Laura had not been interested in sports or exercise. However, as her eating disorder developed, she became more and more involved in exercise as a means to lose weight and as a form of purgation. She became quite proficient at distance running due to her compulsive, excessive exercise. As a result, she began to compete in amateur road races and mini-marathons and often won or placed in these competitions. Unfortunately, her competitions and success provided her with another reason to diet in an effort to maintain a suboptimal weight; she claimed that she had to be thin to be competitive. When Laura sought treatment, her concern was not her eating disorder; rather, she was bothered by relationship difficulties that involved a combination of substance abuse and dissatisfying short-term sexual relationships.

In Laura's case, her involvement with running played a maintenance role in her eating disorder in that it legitimized a suboptimal weight. However, her disorder preceded that involvement. Predisposing factors of unhealthy family dynamics, low self-esteem, perfectionism, and obsessive compulsive traits, as well as impulse control problems in the form of substance abuse and promiscuity, put her at risk for the disorder.

With respect to the maintenance of an eating disorder, dieting's central role involves the individual's inability to get over her disorder as long as she is dieting. As we have discussed and will continue to discuss throughout this book, factors within the sport environment serve to legitimize not only dieting and suboptimal weights but even the eating disorders themselves. Certainly, this is not to imply that most individuals involved with athletes would knowingly encourage an athlete to practice eating-disordered behaviors. Nonetheless, with today's emphasis in sports on lowering body fat to enhance performance, coaches and other individuals who work with athletes may unknowingly encourage them to use pathogenic methods of weight loss. For example, some coaches adopt the attitude that an athlete must compete at a specific weight (optimal competitive weight as defined by the coach) and that the athlete should do whatever it takes to attain and maintain that weight. Unfortunately for some of these athletes, this approach can precipitate an eating disorder or help perpetuate or even exacerbate an existing disorder.

Ideal Body Weight

The term "ideal" usually implies perfection or the ultimate in something. In real life, however, we seldom if ever find anything to be perfect or ultimate. Actually, the term ideal is sometimes used in reference to "ideal body weight" in the medical sense. This has nothing to do with a "perfect" weight. It really refers to recommended weight based on height, body frame, and gender. Even then, ideal body weight is often stated as a weight range.

We sometimes hear athletes or sport-related personnel refer to an "ideal competitive weight." Unfortunately, this has little if anything to do with health. Rather, it suggests that there is a weight—usually a lower weight—at which the participant will be most successful athletically. For example, as one writer on weight control in athletes has reported, "Tables of weight for height, sex, and frame size are of little relevance to the serious athlete. The distance runner will do best when significantly 'underweight' for his or her height when compared with these health standards for the general population" (Smith, 1984, p. 693). In essence, weights below general health standards are sometimes being strongly recommended for athletes.

To think in terms of an ideal weight for sport performance is probably not only unrealistic but also unhelpful in many respects. Interestingly, the individual with an eating problem is usually pursuing the ideal body, shape, or weight. As we have discussed previously, this individual is likely to be quite perfectionistic. Perfection, however, is an illusion that leads to frustration, depression, and poor health. It is important that sport personnel who deal with athletes with eating disorders not contribute to this process by indicating that the athlete should try to attain ideal competitive weight.

Body Fat and Performance

Many coaches and athletes assume that reducing body fat or weight can enhance sport performance. Before discussing this assumption, however, we need to be clear about what reducing body fat means and present some of the facts related to loss of body fat or weight.

Body Weight or Body Fat?

When an athlete is not performing as well as a coach believes he or she should, the coach will look for an explanation and a solution. It is very easy for a coach to notice what looks like fat or extra weight on an athlete. Unfortunately, many coaches decide to have an athlete lose weight based on how the athlete looks. This is not a recommended process in that one cannot always discern body fat by simply looking at the body. It is possible for an individual to look heavy, be heavy, and still have relatively low body fat.

When the coach is making a weight loss decision based on observation alone, is the coach interested in the athlete reducing body weight or body fat? Unfortunately, too many coaches focus on what the scale reads when the athlete is weighed. In this case, the athlete may lose weight but not increase performance. In fact, the athlete may show a decrease in performance due to loss of lean muscle tissue and fluid, for reasons that are explained on pages 49, 79, and 93.

Because of the current emphasis on reducing body fat, many coaches and athletes are becoming more aware of this concept; however, many still have trouble understanding it. To many coaches, reduced body fat means the athlete has less weight to carry and more muscle to work with. Therefore, the athlete should perform better. This simple explanation sounds good and may apply in a small number of cases. But the process of reducing body fat in an attempt to enhance sport performance is actually more complex than it appears. A coach or athlete interested in decreasing the percent body fat is attempting to change body fat composition—that

is, the ratio of body fat to lean tissue. The percent body fat is to be reduced with a resultant increase in the percentage of lean tissue. If weight loss is involved in this process and body fat is lost, the *percentage* of muscle mass increases but the *absolute amount* of muscle in all likelihood decreases due to loss of lean tissue. Researchers have suggested that it is possible to lose weight and preserve lean muscle mass under very controlled circumstances involving a combination of caloric restriction and exercise (McMurray, Ben-Ezra, Forsythe, & Smith, 1985; Pavlou, Steffee, Lerman, & Burrows, 1985). However, body weight loss usually results in a loss of not only body fat but also lean tissue and body fluid.

This process is further complicated by the fact that people interested in weight loss—coaches and athletes in this case—are usually interested in decreasing weight rapidly. Calorie restriction is the fastest way to lose weight and for this reason is often emphasized more. More caloric restriction usually results in greater weight loss but also greater lean tissue loss. And quicker weight loss is usually associated with greater fluid loss. This loss of lean muscle mass and fluid tends to have a negative effect on sport performance. Additionally, negative psychological aspects of the weight loss process that some athletes experience can further detract from sport performance. This is an extremely complex and important issue that will be dealt with in later sections of this book.

Finally, with respect to changing body composition, most coaches and athletes are probably interested in increasing the amount of lean muscle mass. This process does not have to involve weight loss and in all likelihood will increase body weight and body fat as well as lean muscle tissue. Whereas weight loss typically involves a loss of both fat and muscle, weight gain involves an increase in both.

Performance Enhancement

As important as the aforementioned distinctions are in terms of changing body weight or body fat composition, the most important issue involves whether those changes affect sport performance. It appears that they may or may not play a significant role. The relationship between body fat and sport performance is probably more complex than has been assumed, and the importance attached to this relationship has in all likelihood been overstated. Studies in this area are at best equivocal and inconclusive. It is accepted that extra weight requires the use of more muscle fibers, creating a greater oxygen demand by the body when it is exercising. Although this alone can be one indicator of physical fitness that can certainly affect performance, it cannot explain or predict with great accuracy how an athlete will perform.

Whether an athlete is able to enhance performance as a result of weight or body fat loss depends on several factors. Obviously, the higher the level of performance the athlete has achieved before losing body weight or fat, the less effect that loss is likely to have, simply because there is less opportunity for improvement, regardless of weight. For example, a gymnast who consistently scores 9.7 or above on her routines has less opportunity to improve her scores than her teammate who consistently scores below 9.5.

Similarly, the thinner the athlete is before weight loss, the less effect that loss is apt to have. At some point weight loss will produce diminishing returns, for a variety of reasons. For example, a wrestler who is at 8% body fat loses weight in an effort to reduce his body fat composition to 5%. At this point, his weight loss is likely to result in his losing more lean muscle mass and fluid than body fat; loss of either or both of these will decrease his performance.

Also, the type of sport the athlete is involved in may influence whether the athlete's performance is affected by weight or body fat loss. For example, if extra body weight creates more of an oxygen demand on the body, we would expect that athletes in endurance sports like distance running would show the greatest benefit from weight or body fat loss. It would theoretically have less of an effect on athletes' performance in anaerobic sports such as football that require more physical strength and power.

Finally, from a physiological standpoint, the athlete's weight loss practices may determine in part the effect on performance. Weight loss achieved through pathogenic means such as induced vomiting, laxative abuse, or diuretic abuse rather than reasonable eating and exercise regimens will probably have less of a positive effect on performance.

That a relationship exists between body fat and sport performance for many athletes under many circumstances is probably undeniable. At the same time, the exact nature of that relationship is still not fully understood. If weight or body fat loss enhances sport performance, how do we explain average or less-than-average performances by athletes who are at a low weight or low body fat composition? We must conclude that low weight and low body fat are not sufficient for success in sport. Unfortunately, however, many coaches and athletes often view it as such.

We see additional evidence in support of a complex or less than direct relationship between body fat and performance in athletes who are not at a low weight or do not have a low body fat composition but sometimes perform at superior levels. This strongly suggests that thinness or low body fat composition may not only be insufficient for superior sport performance but may not even be necessary for some athletes.

We must keep in mind that for some athletes under some circumstances, weight loss or a reduction in body fat composition *can* lead to improved performance (Wilmore & Costill, 1987). Many athletes, however, will not enhance performance through weight loss. A study by Clark, Nelson, and Evans (1988) with elite middle- and long-distance women runners provides an illustrative example. The investigators found no relationship between racing times and either body weight or body mass index.

Setting Priorities

An important issue regarding lowering body fat or weight has to do with the implicit message that sport performance is more important than the athlete's health. In no situation is this more obvious than the body fat levels that are sometimes recommended in particular sports. Although the average and healthy range is 14% to 16% body fat for young males and 20% to 22% for young females (U.S. Olympic Committee, 1987), many athletes are striving to reach levels significantly lower. Because most young women require at least 17% body fat for the onset of menses to occur (Frisch, 1977), and a higher level (22%) is necessary for regular ovulation (Frisch & McArthur, 1974), this suggests that young women are sacrificing the normal process of menstruation for the sake of possibly enhancing their sport performance. Unfortunately, many athletes not only accept amenorrhea but prefer it in that menstruation may briefly interfere with their training.

Not only are unhealthy body fat levels being recommended by some coaches as well as authors of articles or books devoted to performance in particular sports, many athletes readily accept them as goals they should strive to achieve. This was evidenced when we talked with a group of middle- and long-distance female collegiate runners. When we asked what they thought was a good body fat level to work for, many indicated 10% or less. Interestingly, the coach who was present at this meeting was very surprised by the team's answer. She quickly informed them that their answer was wrong and asked them where they got their information. They responded that this level had been recommended in a popular running magazine.

Finally, and most important from the standpoint of the athlete's physical and psychological well-being, some athletes will respond to dieting and weight loss with eating-disorder symptoms. For these individuals, any positive effects of losing weight or lowering body fat on sport performance will sooner or later be more than offset by the physical and psychological turmoil the weight loss process creates. Although sport performance is important, coaches, trainers, and team physicians should not be distracted by the issue of performance; if reducing body fat or weight places an athlete at greater risk for developing an eating disorder, it doesn't matter that he or she then performs at an elite level.

There are probably exceptions, but sport support staff do not usually allow an athlete to put herself or himself at undue risk of physical injury during conditioning, practicing, or competing. It appears, however, that support staff may not be as careful about health issues related to weight and eating. Why do some coaches and athletic trainers seem to view the development of eating disorders as less serious than other potential medical problems? It may be due purely to a lack of information. More specifically, they may correctly view eating disorders as "emotional" or "psychological" problems but incorrectly assume that they are not "real" problems because they are not physical problems and for this reason are less concerned. Relatedly, they may not feel that these problems are within their area of responsibility as sport personnel. Or they may not feel comfortable or adequate in dealing with psychological problems and therefore try to ignore the problem, hoping they will not have to address it.

In a different vein, some sport personnel may view the issue as one of probability or chance. They may acknowledge that eating disorders are serious problems. However, they may also believe that these disorders do not occur very often. Based on this, they may be willing to take the chance that dieting and weight loss will not lead to eating disorders. Interestingly, they seem less likely to play this probability game with other issues. For example, if we had undeniable evidence that a batter could hit a baseball significantly better if he did not wear a batting helmet, would we allow him to bat without one, even if we knew that the probability of a batter being hit in the head is very low? It is also interesting that for issues related to certain injuries, we have regulations designed to protect the athlete, such as those that prohibit a batter from batting without a helmet. Unfortunately, the only regulations we are aware of regarding weight loss consist of the position statements put forth years ago by the American Medical Association (AMA, 1967) and the American College of Sports Medicine (ACSM, 1976) with respect to weight loss practices of wrestlers, and recent legislation passed in Wisconsin regarding minimum wrestling weights for high school wrestlers. It is also unfortunate that regulations regarding weight are more difficult to enforce. We can see if a batter is not wearing a helmet; the umpire will not allow him to bat until he puts one on. Wrestlers, however, can still employ pathogenic means to quickly reach suboptimal weights, despite the AMA's and ACSM's recommendations and cautions to the contrary.

Special Diagnostic Issues

Because athletes constitute a special population with regard to eating disorders, we need to make special diagnostic considerations when working with athletes. Three of these involve amenorrhea, excessive exercise, and weight criteria. An additional consideration is unhealthy eating and weight loss practices that may appear "normal" or may even be accepted in certain sport circumstances.

Amenorrhea

In the general population, the appropriateness of amenorrhea as a diagnostic criterion is probably questionable on the grounds that it tends to be a result of an eating disorder rather than a cause of it. Its use with athletes, however, involves a different issue. It is sometimes difficult to determine if amenorrhea is a basis for diagnosing a disorder in a female athlete. Amenorrhea in athletes may be more a result of being an athlete than being anorexic. It can be associated with sustained and frequent exercise in athletes whose weight and body fat levels are within normal limits (Kaplan & Woodside, 1987; McArthur et al., 1980). In these cases, the critical factor appears to be low energy intake rather than low weight; that is, these individuals may be burning too many calories through excessive exercise to support their menstrual periods. This may or may not be related to an eating disorder. Additionally, the demands of some sports, whether they are inherent in the sport's activity or made by a coach, may drive the athlete to lower her body fat composition below the level necessary for menses. Finally, it may be difficult to determine the menstrual status of some athletes.

Many women athletes who are actually amenorrheic may be receiving some form of hormone replacement therapy to promote overall health and to reduce the risk of bone density loss in an effort to decrease the likelihood of such injuries as stress fractures. This replacement therapy may be artificially inducing menses in amenorrheic athletes, thereby making the diagnosis of amenorrhea more difficult.

Excessive Exercise

The DSM-III-R (American Psychiatric Association, 1987) criteria for bulimia nervosa includes excessive exercise as a form of purgation. Although this criterion is reasonable and helpful for determining the diagnosis of bulimia nervosa in the general population, it may be less relevant and even misleading when used with athletes. It is quite difficult to distinguish between appropriate and excessive levels of exercise. As difficult as this distinction is in a nonathlete, it is even more difficult in an athlete. Most athletes probably exercise "normally" or appropriately with regard to the training demands for a particular sport or coach. However, what is normal for an athlete often involves a higher level of exercise than for a nonathlete. For example, a college female who is not a varsity athlete but who desperately wants to lose weight runs religiously at least 5 miles every day. She is likely to run more when she believes she has eaten too much. If illness, injury, or other responsibilities interfere with her running, she becomes anxious and agitated. She usually feels guilty when she does not believe she has run enough based on how much she has eaten. Is this individual exercising excessively? Based on her motives for exercise, the intensity of the emotionality she has attached to it, and the fact that she is using it to purge her body of the effects of eating, the answer to this question is probably yes. She may also be eating disordered.

Contrast this with a college distance runner (who may be quite thin) running 75 miles a week as part of her "normal" preparation for the NCAA national championships. She is certainly exercising more than most individuals who are not in her sport, but is she exercising excessively? This must be determined by her motives and feelings regarding her exercise as well as by what constitutes reasonable training given her physical condition and the demands of her sport. If she does not feel compelled to exercise as much as she does, if she is not using running to purge the effects of eating, if she is able to be flexible with her schedule, and if she is not experiencing overuse injuries, then she is probably not exercising excessively.

The important point is that the diagnostic value of exercise has to be evaluated not only within the context of the individual but also within the context of the sport environment. For this reason, it is highly recommended that health care professionals working with athletes be aware of, and experienced with, the "normal" needs, expectations, and demands of the athlete's world. This awareness and experience can be helpful in both diagnosis and treatment.

Weight Criteria

As mentioned in chapter 1, the weight standard typically used for the diagnosis of anorexia nervosa is being at least 15% below an expected or normal body weight. Although this standard is quite helpful in a nonathlete population, like the criterion of excessive exercise it is perhaps less useful with athletes. Many sports emphasize lowering body fat composition in an effort to increase sport performance. As a result, an athlete may be induced by the demands of either a sport or a coach to lose weight to an unhealthy level. Or the athlete may be participating in a sport such as gymnastics, figure skating, or diving that emphasizes form or appearance in its scoring. In either case, the sport may legitimize a low or suboptimal weight; the athlete is apt to cite the weight demand of the sport as the reason for maintaining a body weight below minimal healthy standards rather than a desire to be thin or a fear of becoming "fat." If this is true, is anorexia nervosa the appropriate diagnosis? A key issue is how the athlete in question responds to the concerns of others and their requests for weight gain. If a coach, athletic trainer, physician, or mental health professional tells her that her weight is too low and her health is being compromised, does she agree? Perhaps more important, how does the individual respond when one or all of these people ask her to increase her eating and weight? An individual's responses often indicate the severity of the problem. A positive response may indicate that she is not anorexic—if she admits that she is too thin and does not feel well but is willing to eat more and then follows through with increased food intake, her difficulty is often less serious. But if the athlete in question strongly protests that she cannot or will not eat more because she is already too fat, the problem is apt to be more serious.

Even though we suggest that the diagnostic significance of an athlete's weight may be less clear than that of a nonathlete, this should in no way be construed to mean that the athlete's weight is not important in making a diagnosis. In fact, in some cases it will be the most important diagnostic criterion. We are simply suggesting that the sport environment can affect the individual's weight in several ways, and the sport management team should take these into account when assessing an athlete's eating, weight, and need for treatment.

Other Diagnostic Issues

Other diagnostic issues might include how to handle unusual eating or weight loss practices that are diagnostic of an eating disorder in a nonathlete but not necessarily in an athlete. For example, distance runners may run more than 75 miles a week. They may be 15% below normal body weight and may be very carefully restricting their fat and caloric intake. They may weigh themselves frequently and become concerned with a minimal weight gain. They may find it difficult to take a day off from training. And they may ingest large amounts of carbohydrates the evening before a race. Are they eating disordered? Although these symptoms in nonathletes would often indicate an eating disorder, the issue is much more complex with athletes.

One consideration in attempting to determine the presence or extent of pathology in an athlete's eating regimen or exercise routine involves the demands inherent in a particular sport. As mentioned previously, what looks like excessive exercise may not be excessive when applied in a sport context. For a distance runner to train adequately, he or she must run many miles on a fairly frequent basis. This is not to say that the distance runner can run unlimited miles without the exercise being considered excessive; "excessive" is simply more difficult to determine. Obviously, a probable outcome of significant mileage is weight loss, and that loss may lower the individual's weight to 15% or more below normal body weight. Additionally, individuals convinced that a leaner body will enhance sport performance may become very weight conscious and feel a need to weigh themselves more frequently. This weight-conscious individual, however, may know that carbohydrate loading before a race will provide the glycogen stores necessary for optimal performance and may eat large amounts of pasta the evening before a competition. The behaviors just described may or may not be part of an eating disorder symptom complex; the key word here is "part." Behaviors alone do not constitute a disorder. It is important to remember that eating disorders have not only characteristic behaviors, but also thoughts and emotions that produce the behaviors. If the athlete's thoughts and emotions in a given circumstance are more characteristic of her well-functioning teammates than of individuals with eating disorders, she is probably not eating disordered. For a more thorough discussion of the behaviors, thoughts, and emotions that make up eating disorders as well as the relationship among these components, see Sherman and Thompson (1990).

Diagnostic decisions regarding the extent of eating disturbance in an athlete become more difficult and complex when attitudes and behaviors characteristic of an eating disorder are legitimized by a particular sport. Although excessive exercise, low weight, and weight consciousness are symptoms to be concerned about in nonathletes, in a distance runner they represent attitudes and behaviors that are often accepted and even recommended. As mentioned previously, when one makes a diagnosis it is important to remember the context in which particular behaviors are being exhibited. Although abnormal eating behaviors and attitudes may be normal or expected under a certain set of circumstances, they may not be in the athlete's best interest, either physiologically or psychologically. Consequently, a decision has to be made regarding the potentially unhealthy aspects of the accepted or recommended behavior. This decision has to be made on an individual basis. The criteria for making such a decision involve how the athletically legitimate but nonetheless abnormal eating behaviors and attitudes affect the individual's physical and emotional condition, as well as how they may interfere with everyday functioning.

Wrestling provides an example of how an athlete can practice a behavior considered athletically legitimate that outside the sport would be viewed as abnormal as well as unhealthy. Dropping weight to compete at a lower weight class is common for wrestlers. We know that many wrestlers regularly dehydrate their bodies through various means such as spending excessive time in a sauna or exercising in training clothes that cause excessive sweating. After a period of dieting and dehydration, they may also binge eat. And these behaviors can persist for months. Even though these behaviors are legitimized (accepted) in wrestling, they can nevertheless negatively affect the wrestler's physical and psychological health to the point that they interfere with his ability to perform everyday activities and responsibilities. For example, he may feel so bad physically that he cannot attend his classes. He may be so agitated that he finds himself getting into arguments or even altercations with friends or acquaintances. Or his concentration may be so affected that his studying is unproductive. In such cases, the behaviors in question are creating an untenable situation for the athlete and thus must be eliminated or significantly curtailed, even when an eating disorder is not diagnosed. Treatment may be necessary to bring about this change.

Conclusion

Clearly, athletes compose a special population with regard to eating disorders. They may be more at risk for the development of these disorders for a variety of reasons, some of which reside within the sport environment. Consequently, an effective approach to managing the athlete with an eating disorder will require understanding eating disorders as well as the athlete and the sport environment. In this chapter we examined several commonly held beliefs and attitudes within sport that can contribute to the development of eating disorders in athletes. It appears, however, that this environment may not be the same for all sports or at least that the risk factors may not be as great in some sports as in others. This notion will be more fully developed in chapter 3 as we examine risk factors associated with specific sports.

Specific Sports and Eating Disorders

As we stated earlier, in the general population eating problems occur more frequently in females than in males. Likewise, more female than male athletes have eating problems. Certain sports, however, appear to put both male athletes and female athletes at an even higher risk for developing eating problems. This chapter will examine each of these higher risk sports. Additionally, we will discuss sports or activities that have not been given much attention in terms of research but appear to have characteristics that might place their participants at risk for the development of eating disorders. Due to the disparity in prevalence of eating disorders between female and male athletes, the following discussion of various sports and activities will be divided by gender.

Male Athletes

Before we begin our examination, it might be helpful to speculate as to why male athletes are generally less at risk than female athletes for developing eating disorders. Although this can probably best be explained by gender differences already discussed for the general population, additional explanations may be more specific to sport. One possible explanation involves the current emphasis in sport on low body fat composition. Generally, males have significantly more lean body mass and less body fat than females, especially after puberty. It has been reported that at maturity women have twice as much body fat as men, whereas men have 1.5 times the lean body mass and skeletal mass of women (Rolls, Fedoroff, & Guthrie, 1991; Warren, 1983). Relatedly, males also tend to have a higher metabolic rate because lean tissue is more metabolically active. Rolls et al. suggested that because women have a greater fat-to-lean ratio, a lower metabolic rate, and usually a smaller stature than men, women's energy requirements are less than men's. It is probably easier for women to gain weight and more difficult for them to lose weight than it is for men. As a result, one would predict less of a need for a male athlete to diet to maintain the weight and body fat levels that a coach might recommend or a particular sport might demand. With less of a need to diet, the male athlete's risk of developing an eating disorder is decreased. Evidence of this is provided in a study by Selby, Weinstein, and Bird (1990). In this study of collegiate athletes, more women than men reported difficulty attaining and maintaining their ideal competition weight. They also experienced more negative emotional responses when unable to attain their ideal weight.

Part of the apparent disparity between male and female athletes in terms of prevalence rates of eating disorders may be because such disorders are underreported. Andersen (1990) suggested that for a variety of reasons cases of male athletes with eating disorders are underreported and the statistical scarcity of such disorders in males may make it more difficult for clinicians to recognize them when they do occur. Additionally, he contends that identifying males with eating disorders may be more difficult because special male populations with an increased incidence of eating disorders (i.e., jockeys, wrestlers) probably differ from special female populations (i.e., models). Also, males use different terms than females in expressing conflicts relevant to their disorders. Relatedly, males may be more apt to use exercise to control their weight than the more typical methods women with eating disorders use such as dieting, or diet pills, laxatives, and diuretics. Finally, and perhaps most importantly, males are less likely to present themselves for treatment, regardless of the nature of their psychological difficulty. More specific to eating disorders, they are likely to be even more reluctant to admit to having a "woman's problem."

Most studies investigating eating problems in male athletes have relied on self-report data obtained from the athletes (e.g., Selby et al., 1990; Wilkins et al., 1991). This may explain in part the low rates of eating disturbances or disorders reported for males, given the reasons just discussed regarding underreporting. We will begin our discussion of eating disorders in male athletes in particular sports with an overview of the problem that is provided in a recent survey completed by the NCAA (Dick, 1991), in which data were collected from athletic directors rather than from the athletes themselves. Although this study's data-gathering approach is probably no more methodologically sound than previous studies and has produced results that also undoubtedly underestimate the scope of the problem, it provides an estimate of the prevalence of eating disorders, at least in collegiate athletes, that does not directly rely on athletes' self-report.

The NCAA survey found males with eating disorders in 11 sports. Due to the nature of how data were collected, however, it is difficult to know how many male athletes actually had an eating disorder. Specifically, athletic directors were asked not how many cases there were, but rather in which sports known cases had occurred during a 2-year period. It is probably safe to assume that at least some cases had not been detected by anyone in the sport environment and that some known cases may not have been brought to the attention of the athletic director. Based on this assumption, the survey data probably underrepresent the number of individuals with eating disorders as well as the number of schools and sports from which these individuals come. Even with underreporting, 67 NCAA member institutions reported the presence of at least one male athlete with anorexia nervosa or bulimia. When we combine the expected underreporting for methodological reasons in this study with the purported underreporting of eating disorders in male athletes for other reasons, we must conclude that the problem of eating disorders in male athletes is probably greater than it appears to be. We should keep this in mind as we discuss specific sports believed to place male athletes at risk.

Wrestling

Wrestlers constitute the one group of male athletes most often mentioned as a population at risk for sports-induced eating disturbances. This at-risk status appears well deserved based on data obtained in the NCAA survey mentioned previously (Dick, 1991). Of the 67 schools reporting the presence of an eating disorder in a particular sport, 20 involved wrestling. The reason wrestling appears to place wrestlers at risk for developing an eating disorder is that many wrestlers compete in weight classes that are 15 pounds or more below their off-season weight. In this regard, Steen and

Brownell (1990) found that the majority of the college wrestlers and a third of the high school wrestlers in their survey reported difficulty in making weight. It is not unusual for wrestlers in this situation to deprive themselves of food and water to make their weight standard. Other common weight-loss techniques wrestlers employ include laxative and diuretic abuse, excessive exercise, and thermal methods such as sauna use and wearing rubber suits (Steen & Brownell, 1990; Steen & McKinney, 1986).

Tipton, Tcheng, and Paul (1969) found that a typical weight loss for a wrestler will involve a 2% to 12% change in body weight 2 to 48 hours before competition. Following either the weigh-in for a match or the match itself, it is not uncommon for wrestlers to engage in eating that they perceive as out of control (Steen & Brownell, 1990). More specifically, many wrestlers overeat or binge eat in response to the restrictive dieting and deprivation they have endured while attempting to make weight. In essence, many wrestlers are engaged in a cycle of rapid and dramatic weight loss followed by weight restoration or weight gain. Wrestlers may repeat these weight loss–binge-eating cycles as often as 30 times throughout a season.

In comparing wrestlers who had engaged in repeated cycles of weight loss and regain to those who had not, Steen, Oppliger, and Brownell (1988) found that the weight-cycling wrestlers' resting metabolic rate was 14% lower. Because dieting may enhance food efficiency (decrease metabolism), weight loss occurs more slowly and weight gain more rapidly with each successive diet. It has been suggested that the weight cycling that wrestlers engage in is apt to make losing weight more and more difficult for them as their careers progress (Garner & Rosen, 1991). More important, however, are the findings of a recent study suggesting that weight cycling through dietary means may play a role in the development of coronary heart disease (Lissner et al., 1991).

It is probably safe to assume that the process just described becomes difficult for the individual to manage as he ages. Sport competition eventually ceases for most athletes, and a normal lowering of activity level and metabolism occurs with age. As a consequence, we would expect weight gain to continue. Such was the case for a former collegiate wrestler at 190 pounds who sought treatment for an eating disorder. In the 5 years after the end of competitive wrestling, he had weight cycled numerous times, with his weight reaching a high of 280 pounds. His eating and weight history was replete not only with numerous diets but also periods of bulimia and what he called "compulsive eating," which in actuality involved binge eating without purging.

Weight gain is not the only consequence of wrestlers' repeated unhealthy weight loss measures. It has been suggested that the weight-cutting practices wrestlers use may impair growth and development (Steen & Brownell, 1990). Also, most of the weight lost using pathogenic means results from dehydration. Dehydration and rapid weight loss cause changes in the body that put the athlete at risk for medical difficulties. Fluid losses can influence cardiac output, temperature regulation, electrolyte stability, and possible renal changes (Brownell, Steen, & Wilmore, 1987). Additionally, Strauss, Lanese, and Malarkey (1985) found low serum testosterone levels in wrestlers, especially when body fat dropped below 5%. Webster, Rutt, and Weltman (1990) found that the use of these pathogenic weight loss methods (primarily dehydration) resulted in a reduction in upper body strength measures as well as in a deleterious effect on anaerobic power, anaerobic capacity, the lactate threshold, and aerobic power. Finally, most wrestlers not only try to lose weight, they also attempt to change their lean-to-fat ratio to increase strength and performance. Ironically, the severe dieting they engage in can cause loss of lean muscle mass that most often is not replaced completely when weight is regained. This can lead to slight alterations in the lean-to-fat ratio with each weight loss–weight gain cycle (Brownell et al., 1987), but not in the direction intended.

Although many of these studies are relatively recent, the health consequences of weight cutting by wrestlers was addressed much earlier by the American College of Sports Medicine (ACSM, 1976). The ACSM warned against the common practice of "making weight" through food restriction, fluid deprivation, and dehydration. Specifically, it reported that these practices generally cause a reduction in muscular strength, a decrease in work performance times, lower plasma and blood volumes, a reduction in cardiac functioning during submaximal work conditions that are associated with high heart rates, smaller stroke volumes and reduced cardiac outputs, lower oxygen consumption, an impairment of thermoregulatory processes, a decrease in renal blood flow and in the volume of fluid being filtered by the kidney, a depletion of liver glycogen stores, and an increase in the amount of electrolytes being lost from the body. The ACSM therefore discourages severe weight reduction and has provided guidelines to eliminate the current procedures of making weight.

The most disconcerting part of our current state of knowledge is that despite the admonitions of researchers and sports medicine professionals regarding the use of pathogenic weight loss methods, it appears that these methods are still commonly practiced by wrestlers (Steen & Brownell, 1990). We know that certain health complications are associated with wrestlers' disturbed eating behaviors. We also know that these complications can negatively affect sport performance. But are the pathogenic methods of weight control wrestlers use related to the development of eating disorders? In the NCAA survey (Dick, 1991) cited earlier, 20 (7%) of the schools sponsoring wrestling indicated the presence of at least one case of an eating disorder. Nonetheless, in a study by Enns, Drewnowski, and Grinker (1987), the Eating Attitudes Test (EAT; Garner & Garfinkel, 1979) was administered to a group of collegiate wrestlers. The EAT is a measure of behaviors associated with anorexia nervosa, including avoidance of fatness, binge eating, purging, and the use of strenuous exercise as a means to control weight (Garner & Garfinkel, 1979). The investigators found that 21% of the wrestlers scored higher than the typical score used for referral for a clinical interview. Although these individuals scored particularly high on items associated with a drive for thinness, all denied vomiting or using laxatives as means to control weight. Based on these data, it would be difficult to conclude that these individuals had eating disorders. It appears that even though many, even most, wrestlers engage in dieting and pathogenic weight loss behaviors, the majority are probably able to return to eating normally during the off-season. Still, at least some of these individuals might benefit from nutritional and psychological counseling. Wrestlers who dehydrate themselves prior to the weigh-in before a match probably will not experience or exhibit enough characteristics of an eating disorder to warrant a formal diagnosis. Some, however, may actually be practicing a subclinical variant of anorexia nervosa or bulimia nervosa that might eventually develop into the full clinical disorder without some form of intervention. An assessment or evaluation by an eating disorder treatment specialist would certainly be appropriate for wrestlers for whom there is the slightest concern.

Distance Running

Besides wrestlers, distance runners have received the most attention and investigation regarding eating disorders in male athletes. A controversial article by Yates, Leehey, and Shisslak (1983) suggested that obligatory runners resembled patients with anorexia nervosa in a variety of psychological traits and behaviors. Specifically, they found that in their sample, male runners were preoccupied with weight and body fat, followed rigid diets, and increased running distance to compensate for overeating. In addition, they found that the two groups shared personality traits, including inhibition of anger, perfectionism, tolerance of physical discomfort, and tendencies toward depression. This study spawned a series of related investigations due to criticisms that the original study was not scientifically controlled or sound. These subsequent investigations suggested that male runners and women with anorexia nervosa are not similar in psychopathology (Blumenthal, O'Toole, & Chang, 1984; Nudelman, Rosen, & Leitenberg, 1988). Nudelman and colleagues found that "male runners are not anxious about eating, are not overly preoccupied with food, do not engage in excessive binge-eating or purging behavior, are not negatively preoccupied with their weight, are not intent on losing weight, do not possess the personality traits presumed to underlie eating disorders, and are not depressed or low in self-esteem" (p. 631). They noted, however, that their results were based on average results and that does not mean there are no individual high-intensity runners with symptoms of an eating disorder.

Intuitively, one would expect distance running to place males at risk for the development of eating disorders based on the lean shape believed to be necessary for optimal performance in that sport, especially at elite levels. Dick (1991) reported that 3% of the NCAA schools sponsoring cross-country indicated the presence of at least one case of an eating disorder. Although this is in all likelihood an underestimation of the prevalence of eating disorders in cross-country participants, a high incidence of eating disorders has yet to be found. Likewise, a relationship between distance running in males and increased risk for the development of an eating disorder has not been determined empirically.

Horse Racing

Although it has often been suggested that jockeys are apt to constitute a group at risk for the development of eating disorders (Andersen, 1990; Garner & Rosen, 1991; Mickalide, 1990; Root, Fallon, & Friedrich, 1986), little research has actually investigated this. The only study in this area (King & Mezey, 1987) is fraught with methodological difficulties related to sampling and data collection, and thus any inferences drawn from it should be taken with caution. In this study, 10 jockeys who agreed to be interviewed completed a series of instruments designed to elicit information regarding psychiatric and eating symptoms. Current weights were found to be 13% below matched population mean weights. All jockeys reported a wide range of weight-control methods. Most reported the use of dehydration, strenuous exercise, fasting, laxatives, or diuretics to lose weight. Two jockeys reported using appetite suppressants, whereas one admitted to self-induced vomiting. Six reported binge eating, usually following "wasting" or losing weight. Despite these findings, the investigators concluded on the basis of interview data analysis that no cases of an eating disorder were found.

Even though this study suffers from methodological problems, its findings suggest that jockeys may be induced to use pathogenic weight loss methods to achieve suboptimal weights to maintain their livelihood. Further investigation of this group is necessary to determine whether the use of such methods places jockeys at increased risk for the development of anorexia or bulimia nervosa.

Livelihood and Weight Control

Professional athletes in sports requiring weight control sometimes must face the issue of livelihood. A jockey who does not keep his weight down will have fewer opportunities to ride. Fewer opportunities to ride mean fewer opportunities to make money practicing his chosen profession. Are professional athletes in sports requiring weight control more likely to diet or be willing to engage in pathogenic weight loss methods than amateur athletes who are not being compensated financially based on performance? The answer to this question is probably yes, because financial compensation is simply another inducement to diet. The role that financial compensation plays as an inducement to diet or maintain a low weight in professional athletes warrants further investigation.

Bodybuilding

Although little research has been done in this sport, bodybuilding appears to possibly put its competitors at risk for developing eating disorders. Bodybuilding is an appearance sport in which the primary goal is to significantly increase lean muscle mass and decrease body fat to present a very well-defined, muscular form. Scoring is dependent on judges' ratings of appearance. Additionally, the training for bodybuilding is primarily anaerobic, which means the athlete has little opportunity to control his weight through running or some other form of aerobic activity. This in all likelihood increases the risk that bodybuilders will use dieting or forms of weight manipulation to control or lose weight. Relatedly, steroid use has apparently been an accepted part of the sport. If bodybuilders are willing to take risks associated with steroid use, it is plausible to assume that they would also engage in pathogenic body and weight manipulations—manipulations that might significantly affect performance in other sports. Even though training in bodybuilding requires strenuous, extensive exercise, bodybuilding competitions require only appearance. Because competition—appearance in this case—is not apt to be visibly affected by pathogenic means of weight manipulation, participants might be more willing to experiment with pathogenic weight loss methods just before a contest.

The few investigations involving bodybuilders have produced inconclusive results. In a study by Pasman and Thompson (1988), no distinction was made between obligatory weight lifters who were bodybuilders and those who were power lifters. These groups have different weight-related goals. As mentioned previously, bodybuilders are concerned with appearance. Power lifters are more concerned with adding bulk to increase strength and power. Also, the subjects included both males and females, although findings indicated that they were similar on most measures. Nonetheless, results indicated that the lifters had a higher level of eating disturbance than controls for some anorexic tendencies but not for bulimic behaviors. They did not, however, engage in the body distortion that is characteristic of anorexia patients.

Conclusion

In all likelihood, eating disorders in male athletes have been underreported. This means that many affected male athletes have not received the treatment they need. Thus, it is important that we not assume that because 90% of the individuals with eating disorders are women, we do not need to be concerned about men being at risk.

Female Athletes

Certainly, eating disorders can be found in female athletes in all sports. The recent NCAA survey (Dick, 1991) received 810 reports of eating disorders in 15 sports. Eating disorders are not, however, equally distributed among sports. Depending on the individual and her sport, a relationship may or may not exist between the disorder and the sport. As mentioned previously, being part of a group or engaging in an activity that emphasizes a particular small size, thin shape, or low weight increases an athlete's risk of developing an eating disorder. For this reason, athletes in sports or activities that focus on form in their scoring (i.e., diving, gymnastics, figure skating) or emphasize a thin, lean body (i.e., ballet, distance running) would appear to be at higher risk for the development of an eating disorder. This contention is in part borne out by the NCAA study mentioned earlier. In this survey, gymnastics, cross-country, and track (running events) were the sports that most often reported having at least one athlete with an eating disorder. Specifically, 48%, 23%, and 21% of the schools sponsoring gymnastics, cross-country, and track, respectively, reported at least one athlete with an eating disorder. On the other hand, with diving, only 6% of the sponsoring schools reported at least one athlete with an eating disorder.

In a more empirical study, Borgen and Corbin (1987) compared women athletes in sports emphasizing leanness with those in other sports on the Eating Disorder Inventory (EDI; Garner, Olmsted, & Polivy, 1983). They found that individuals participating in activities that emphasized leanness—ballet, bodybuilding, cheerleading, and gymnastics—more often had EDI scores more similar to or above those of anorexics than were the EDI scores of athletes in activities with no emphasis on leanness (swimming, track and field, and volleyball). The investigators' choice to include swimming and track as non-leanness sports is confusing in light of recent evidence that suggests these activities may have relatively high rates of eating disorders, in part because they do emphasize leanness or low body fat. For this reason, it is difficult to determine whether the results are in any way meaningful.

In a similar but less confounded study, Davis and Cowles (1989) compared athletes from activities for which a thin body build (TB) was viewed as advantageous (gymnastics, synchronized swimming, diving, figure skating, distance running, and ballet) with athletes from sports not stressing a thin body build. Findings indicated that the TB group had a greater drive for thinness, was significantly thinner, and had fewer menstrual periods. The TB athletes were also less extroverted, tended to be less stable, and reported a lower sense of emotional well-being.

Even though differences have sometimes been found between athletes from "thinness-demand" sports and athletes from sports not stressing thinness, the differences have not always indicated a difference in terms of prevalence of eating disorders. Brooks-Gunn, Burrow, and Warren (1988) compared competitive adolescent athletes in the thinness-demand activities of figure skating and ballet with swimmers and a nonathlete comparison group with regard to attitudes toward eating and body weight. As expected, findings indicated that the skaters and dancers were lighter and leaner than the swimmers and had higher eating-problem scores. Nonetheless, only 5% of the dancers and none of the other athletes had clinically high scores on the Eating Attitudes Test (EAT).

Although there may be some question as to the exact nature of the relationship between thinness-demand sports and eating disorders, there is little question that the female gymnast is viewed both inside and outside the sport as the athlete most at risk for the development of an eating disorder. Because of the high rates of eating-related problems purported to exist in this group of athletes, probably no other athlete has been investigated as thoroughly in this area as the female gymnast.

Gymnastics

Gymnastics requires not only strength, flexibility, and coordination but also grace. Aesthetics play an important role in competition. Currently, that means in part placing a premium on thinness. At the same time, gymnastics is primarily an anaerobic sport, which means that athletes do not expend the same high levels of energy (burn as many calories) as in endurance sports like running. With the emphasis on appearance and thinness and without aerobic training to aid in weight maintenance, it is easy to understand why so many gymnasts focus on their weight and rely on caloric restriction to attain and maintain a low weight. One study by Rosen and Hough (1988), for example, found that all of the gymnasts they surveyed (n = 42) were actively dieting. In addition, 62% were using at least one form of pathogenic weight control such as self-induced vomiting, diet pills, fasting, diuretics, fluid restriction, or laxatives. They also found that those athletes who were told by their coaches that they were too heavy were more likely to resort to pathogenic weight-control methods. In fact, coaches told two-thirds of these gymnasts that they were too heavy, and 75% of those athletes did resort to these dangerous weight-control behaviors. Of the one-third who were not told they were too heavy, 36% still resorted to pathogenic weight loss methods.

Do gymnasts really need to be as thin as many of them strive to be to be successful in their sport? The answer is probably yes, especially at elite levels. There appear to be at least two components to this need to be thin. One relates to a particular body size and shape that facilitates the performance of gymnastic skills. The very small, prepubescent shape may allow for easier maneuverability in certain gymnastic movements or on particular apparatus. The second component pertains to appearance. Many gymnastics coaches and competitors believe that judges' scoring is affected by the gymnast's shape. More specifically, a gymnast with a thin, almost shapeless form is believed to receive higher scores because of her straight-line appearance.

If gymnasts and their coaches believe that a thin shape can enhance performance and positively affect judges' scoring, we would expect to find female gymnasts dieting for one or both of these reasons, and this is in fact the case. With respect to performance, Falls and Humphrey (1978) found that those gymnasts who earned

medals in a national gymnastics meet by placing first, second, or third had significantly lower body fat than those who did not place. A study by Rosen and Hough (1988) is even more illustrative. These researchers found not only that half the gymnasts in their study were dieting to enhance performance, but also that the other half were dieting to improve their appearance. Interestingly, as convinced as coaches and gymnasts seem to be that a thin shape results in higher scores, no controlled study has determined the optimal weight-to-height ratios for peak gymnastic performance.

Despite the emphasis on low body weight and the number of gymnasts who diet, only very few of them approach dieting in a systematic, healthful way. Costar (1983) found that just 7% of his sample of gymnasts were following a formal diet prescribed by a physician or trainer. In a study of 13 elite high school gymnasts, Moffatt (1984) found that 9 were eating less than 100% of the RDA (recommended daily allowance for nutrients), 5 were eating less than 75% of the RDA, and one was eating less than 40%. Similarly, Coleman (1986) reported that 30% of the gymnasts she surveyed consumed foods that provided less than 50% of the RDA, and 60% ingested less than 80% of the RDA for at least one nutrient. These findings underscore the apparent problem of nutritional deficiency in gymnasts resulting from restrictive dieting.

Diving

Although very little research has been done concerning divers and eating disorders, we believe that as a group of athletes they are also at risk for developing eating problems. This is due in part to the sport's demand for a lean body. It has been suggested that the ideal body fat range for an elite female diver is 8% to 14% (as compared to 20% to 22% for the average young female) and that fat weight detracts from performance and appearance (Eisenman, 1990). Because diving is a water sport, researchers have sometimes mistakenly grouped divers with swimmers. However, the demands of diving are actually quite close to those of gymnastics. As in gymnastics, participants and coaches believe that judges' scoring is affected by the diver's shape. Also like gymnastics, diving is primarily an anaerobic activity that does not provide the athlete with much opportunity to burn off calories while placing a premium on a long and slender shape.

No study has looked specifically at divers and their eating patterns. The study discussed previously by Davis and Cowles (1989) measured weight and diet concerns as well as personality factors in divers and athletes in five other thin-build sports. Because the results were reported for the entire group of athletes, we still know little about the specific needs or issues of divers. We do know, however, that divers must contend with many issues that apparently have put other athletes at risk. In addition, they must train and perform in very small, revealing bathing suits that in essence put their bodies on display. This display takes place not only in front of spectators at competitions but also during practices, allowing divers to compare their own body sizes and shapes unfavorably with those of other divers. For these reasons, we believe divers are likely to be at high risk for eating disturbances.

Distance Running

Researchers interested in eating disorders in athletes have paid much attention to female distance runners. Much of this attention was generated by an article by Yates et al. (1983) that compared male distance runners with anorexic patients. Even though many researchers (i.e., Nudelman et al., 1988) have legitimately criticized the methodology and conclusions of Yates and her associates, the study has nonetheless stimulated investigators to look at distance runners and their potential for developing eating disorders. Weight and Noakes (1987) tested the hypothesis of Yates et al. on a sample of female marathon and cross-country runners. They concluded that abnormal eating attitudes and the incidence of anorexia nervosa is no more common in competitive female runners than it is in the general population. They speculated as did Gadpaille et al. (1987), however, that some women who are predisposed to developing anorexia nervosa use running as a substitute vehicle, and doing so sufficiently satisfies them so they do not develop the full-blown clinical disorder. Owens and Slade (1987) likewise found that although anorexia nervosa is found in distance runners, no evidence exists that the incidence in runners is higher than in the normal population.

Unfortunately, not all research in this area has been so optimistic. In a study of the nutritional status of elite female distance runners, Clark et al. (1988) found a history of anorexia nervosa in 13% of their sample. They also found that most of the women appeared to be very weight conscious, and many were eating fewer calories, and consequently fewer nutrients, than they needed for proper nutrition. The authors' concern was that the athletes' inadequate diets may predispose them to amenorrhea, stress fractures, and possibly other injuries. Their results justified this concern: Seventy-two percent of the amenorrheic group reported having at least one stress fracture, as compared to 36% of the runners who were menstruating. In addition, multiple stress fractures were reported by 50% of the amenorrheic runners but by only 9% of those regularly menstruating.

The relationship between eating disorders and amenorrhea has been a focus in other research with distance runners. In a study investigating the relationship between eating disorders, athletic amenorrhea, and major affective or depressive disorders, Gadpaille et al. (1987) conducted psychiatric interviews with 13 amenorrheic and 19 regularly menstruating runners. Eight amenorrheic runners (62%) reported eating disorders in themselves as compared to none in the menstruating group. Also, three (23%) of the amenorrheic runners reported major depressive disorders as compared to none in the menstruating group. Depressive disorders were even more common among relatives of the amenorrheic group (77%), whereas they occurred in only one relative (5%) of the menstruating group. Based on these results, the investigators speculated that some cases of athletic amenorrhea, eating disorders, and major depression may constitute biologically and genetically related conditions.

Some studies with female distance runners have looked at attitudes and behaviors characteristic of individuals with eating disorders rather than at the prevalence of actual clinical disorders. For example, Rosen et al. (1986) found that almost half of their sample of female distance runners (8 of 17) used at least one pathogenic weight-control behavior. Five of the 8 engaged in self-induced vomiting, 3 abused laxatives, and 6 took diet pills. Most of the athletes surveyed indicated that their concern about weight was related primarily to sport performance rather than to enhancing their appearance. Pasman and Thompson (1988) found that female distance runners were much more dissatisfied with their bodies than were male distance runners. Although the use of pathogenic weight loss methods and body dissatisfaction are characteristics often found in individuals with eating disorders, they are not necessarily diagnostic of an actual disorder. It is probably safe to assume, however, that they place the athlete at greater risk for developing an eating disorder.

As we might expect, the distance runner's risk for developing eating disturbances or disorders is related to her need to be thin for her sport. This need to be thin—that is, the reason for dieting—is related to the strongly held belief among distance runners that the thinner they are, the faster and better they will be able to run. Although many runners and their coaches are convinced of this relationship, the literature in this area is inconclusive. A study by Wilmore, Brown, and Davis (1977) recorded body fat measures for 70 female distance runners. The variability of body fat composition and running performance of four of the best runners is illustrative. The two leanest (with approximately 6% body fat) were two of the most successful. On the other hand, one of the other two highly successful runners had 17% body fat, and the other had the highest percent body fat in the group—35.8%.

The study by Clark et al. (1988) provides more evidence to challenge the belief that low body fat enhances running performance. Clark and her associates found no relationship between the fastest racing times and either body weight or body mass index (BMI) in the 93 elite distance runners they studied.

The prevalence of eating disorders in distance runners is unclear. Some studies find a higher incidence of eating disorders, yet others find no differences. We do know that the incidence of amenorrhea is higher in distance runners than in the general population, and we also know that amenorrhea puts athletes at risk for other problems (e.g., stress fractures and possibly depression, as well as other medical problems). Finally, as noted earlier, some have suggested that running may serve as an outlet for women who might otherwise have developed anorexia nervosa. This notion has not been scientifically documented, however, and is based primarily on conjecture. One way to investigate this would be to look at injured runners. If running serves as a buffer against the development of an eating disorder, we would expect eating disorder symptoms to emerge in at-risk runners (those predisposed to develop such a disorder) when injuries prevent them from running. Obviously, there is much more we need to understand about eating problems and distance running.

Swimming

Traditionally, swimming has not been thought of as a thinness-demand sport. In fact, in studies comparing different sports with respect to eating disorder characteristics, researchers have often called it an activity that does not emphasize leanness (e.g., Benson, Alleman, Theintz, & Howald, 1990; Borgen & Corbin, 1987). Nonetheless, eating problems in swimmers have been documented. Twenty-one percent of the schools in the NCAA survey (Dick, 1991) sponsoring women's swimming reported at least one case of an eating disorder.

Investigations of swimming have often produced evidence that its participants display attitudes and behaviors characteristic of individuals with eating problems, but no clear indication of the prevalence of actual clinical disorders has emerged. For example, a study by Dummer et al. (1987) found that young (9–18 years) competitive female swimmers were likely to misperceive themselves as overweight. Additionally, 39.9% of the girls reported that they often or almost always worried about their weight, and 15.4% (24.8% of the postmenarcheal girls) used pathogenic weight loss methods. They also listed appearance as their most important reason for losing weight. Similarly, Rosen et al. (1986) found that one of nine swimmers surveyed engaged in pathogenic weight-control behaviors. In a study looking at female adolescent Swiss athletes, Benson et al. (1990) found 11% of the swimmers to be exceptionally preoccupied with weight, and 38% scored high on body dissatisfaction as measured by the EDI. Based on EDI scores and other self-reported measures of eating characteristics, we (Sherman & Thompson, 1991) found swimmers as a group to be at higher risk for eating disturbances than most other collegiate sport groups or teams in our survey.

Even though these studies do not look at the prevalence of eating disorders per se in swimmers, the findings indicate that female swimmers often report attitudes and behaviors characteristic of individuals with eating disorders. Why would a sport that supposedly does not emphasize leanness place its participants at apparently high risk for eating disturbances? Swimming may present a unique set of pressures that result in a swimmer's perceived need to lose weight. Although swimming is not an appearance sport, swimmers, like divers, spend a great deal of time in bathing suits, often in front of large crowds. Although after a while some swimmers may be able to desensitize themselves in this regard, others may not and thus may feel a need to lose weight for appearance reasons. As with divers, being in bathing suits allows athletes frequent opportunities to compare body sizes and shapes, resulting in more weight preoccupation or body dissatisfaction. Additionally, some swimmers also attempt to reduce body fat to enhance performance. Thus, some swimmers are apt to feel the pressure to lose weight for both appearance and performance reasons. Finally, the energy expenditure required in advanced levels of the sport may dictate that a swimmer eat large amounts of food during the season. Although this is necessary and helpful during the competitive season, it may make it difficult for the swimmers to reduce food intake during the off-season, when training is less intensive and energy expenditure significantly less. Several of the swimmers we talked with report that their eating problems began as a result of weight gain during the off-season.

Figure Skating

Figure skating is sometimes mentioned as a high-risk sport for eating disorders (e.g., Garner & Rosen, 1991), probably because, much like gymnastics, it is an appearance sport that relies on judges' scoring, and participants purportedly emphasize leanness to enhance their performance. Even more of a weight concern may exist in pairs competition than in singles, because the female skater must be lifted by her male partner. Figure skating has been given little attention in the literature, however. In a study discussed earlier (Brooks-Gunn et al., 1988) comparing figure skaters with ballet dancers, swimmers, and a control group, figure skaters were found to be most like dancers. They tended to be leaner and lighter than both swimmers and the control group and had a later menarcheal age. Skaters also scored higher than swimmers but lower than dancers on the EAT subscale Dieting, Bulimia, Oral Control, as well as on the EDI subscale Perfectionism. When compared to dancers, skaters had lower dieting and higher oral control scores. Brooks-Gunn et al. suggested that their results may reflect the demands for low weight in ballet and figure skating. In the Davis and Cowles study (1989), figure skaters were part of a group of thin body-build athletes that was compared to a normal-build athlete group with regard to eating disorder indicators, weight and dieting concerns, and personality factors. Although data specific to skaters were not available, their group showed a greater drive for thinness, was significantly thinner, and had fewer menstrual cycles than the other group. In the one study that looked specifically at figure skaters, Rucinski (1989) investigated the relationship between body image and dietary intake. Results indicated that the female skaters' caloric intake was well below the RDAs for moderately active individuals. Also, 48% recorded EAT scores of 30 or higher, which indicate eating attitudes similar to those of anorexics.

As in other sports that take place at the professional level, eating problems or at least the pressure to diet to maintain a particular shape may be even greater for professional skaters. One former skater suggested that the emphasis in ice shows is more on appearance than performance. She told us that professional skaters sometimes were docked pay for being overweight.

Dancing

Even though dancers may not be considered athletes in the true sense of the term, dancing can certainly be considered an athletic activity. Like gymnasts, dancers place a premium on a slim body shape; also, a dancer's daily training regimen typically has a smaller aerobic component that does not involve the caloric expenditure of endurance sports like running or swimming. The combination of a demand for a thin shape without endurance training increases the need for dieting, which puts the dancer at risk for developing an eating disorder. Garner, Garfinkel, Rockert, and Olmsted (1987) looked at 55 female ballet students age 11 to 14 in a highly competitive ballet school and found that more than 25% showed evidence of an eating disorder, a figure significantly higher than in the general population. Likewise, Szmukler, Eisler, Gillies, and Hayward (1985) found significant eating disturbances in their sample of 100 adolescent female ballet students in London. Rates among professional dancers are probably higher. We mentioned earlier that professional athletes such as jockeys and figure skaters feel tremendous pressure to maintain a low weight to be financially successful in their chosen livelihoods. Professional dancers are apt to feel these same pressures. Additionally, it is likely that for the professional dancer, dancing is not merely her livelihood; it is the most important thing in her life and probably has been since early childhood. As a consequence, she may feel that she has no choice—she must do whatever it takes to maintain a low weight.

Eating disorders begin with a diet, and many dancers are frequently (and perhaps constantly) dieting. Calabrese et al. (1983) found that in 34 high-level classical ballet dancers, just 71.6% of the RDA for nutrients was consumed. And 46% of their sample were consuming less than 66% of the RDA. The average percent body fat in their sample was 16.9%, which is much lower than that seen in women who are not dancers. Finally, they found a considerable number of menstrual abnormalities.

In addition to the high risk for developing eating disorders and menstrual difficulties, the poor nutrition and high degree of food *faddism* (Calabrese et al., 1983) found in dancers also puts them at high risk for numerous injuries and stress fractures. Frusztajer, Dhuper, Warren, Brooks-Gunn, and Fox (1990) found that the majority (80%) of the dancers they surveyed with recent stress fractures weighed less than 75% of their ideal weight. Additionally, this group showed a greater incidence of eating disorders when compared to a group of dancers without stress fractures. As might be expected, this group also had a lower fat intake and a higher intake of low-calorie food.

One study compared modern dance students and ballerinas to determine the impact of different types of dance on the development of eating disorders (Schnitt, Schnitt, & Del A'une, 1986). The sample of modern dance students in this study had more normal eating patterns than did groups of student ballerinas studied and reported in the literature. Even so, all of the 62 modern dance students were below the expected body weight (EBW) for their heights (as calculated from the 1983 Metropolitan height and weight tables), and the average body weight for the group was 88.1% EBW. In addition, 8 of the 62 dancers had EAT scores of 30 or more, which is highly suggestive of anorexia nervosa, and another 8 scored between 25 and 30 on the EAT, which is in the borderline area. When compared to ballet dancers in previous studies, this sample of modern dancers showed a higher percentage of expected body weight and lower EAT scores. The investigators suggested that even though their sample of modern dancers did not show anorexic attitudes as frequently as ballet dancers, a subpopulation of modern dancers is probably at risk for anorexia nervosa or anorexic-like attitudes.

Cheerleading

Like dancers, cheerleaders are certainly athletic, but it might be debatable whether they are in fact athletes. Nonetheless, the activity of cheerleading, as well as the appearance demands associated with it, probably make it a high-risk activity for eating disorders. Even though some researchers (e.g., Borgen & Corbin, 1987; Burckes-Miller & Black, 1988) have surveyed cheerleaders as part of a larger group of athletes, few have looked exclusively at this group. One study that did (Lundholm & Littrell, 1986) surveyed 751 high school female cheerleaders and found that those who expressed a strong desire for thinness had significantly higher scores on seven of eight eating-disorder scales.

The demand for thinness in cheerleaders is clearly indicated by the weight policies that many cheerleading programs have established. Whether these policies reflect an emphasis on weight for ease of maneuverability during stunts or simply for appearance is unclear. A recent policy outlined by a nationally prominent collegiate program not only proposed a weight standard of 120 pounds as an upper limit for female cheerleaders, but also declared that body fat composition levels were to be between 9% and 17%. Unfortunately, at this level of body fat, most young women will not be able to have normal menstrual cycles. Interestingly, this weight policy was designed at least in part to prevent and detect eating disorders, which is admirable. At the same time, however, the policy stated that "squad members who acknowledge an eating disorder problem shall be suspended from performance" and that "A squad member whose eating-disorder problem presents sufficient documented disruption to squad practice, travel, and performance may be suspended or terminated from the program." It is doubtful that a cheerleader in such a program would risk being suspended from the squad by admitting to having an eating disorder. In fact, this type of policy would probably ensure that a cheerleader with an eating disorder would *not* report her disorder.

Bodybuilding

Intuitively, we might think that bodybuilding appears to put female athletes at risk for developing eating disorders, although no empirical data exist to support such a claim. We have already examined the aspects of bodybuilding that place athletes at risk in our discussion of male bodybuilders. In addition to these, Yates (1991) contends that women bodybuilders have to train longer and harder than men and diet more diligently to reduce their higher levels of body fat. She also suggests that they must take diuretics to reduce body fluids to show the vein-rippled effect that reportedly scores well with judges. Yates's contentions would imply that female bodybuilders are probably at greater risk than their male counterparts. However, in the Pasman and Thompson (1988) study discussed earlier, female weight lifters (both bodybuilders and power lifters) reported no greater body dissatisfaction than the male weight lifters, a finding that runs counter not only to other sports but to the general population as well.

Unfortunately, much of our present knowledge about the prevalence of eating disorders in bodybuilders is based on anecdotal information and on a small number of studies that have incorporated bodybuilders into a larger sample of athletes. Studies that look specifically at the eating-related attitudes and behaviors of bodybuilders are obviously needed. Nonetheless, what we do know indicates that even though these athletes may not be at risk for developing actual disorders, they are probably at risk for using restrictive dieting, pathogenic weight loss methods, and excessive exercise.

Conclusion

At the beginning of our discussion of female athletes, we stated that all sports have athletes with eating disorders. Whereas eating disorders among athletes in thinness-demand sports in many cases appear to be either directly or indirectly related to their sport, reports of athletes with eating disturbances in other sports suggest that their disorders are less likely to be sport related. As a result, the rates of eating difficulties in non-thinness-demand sports appear to be no greater than rates found in the general population. For example, basketball, volleyball, tennis, golf, and softball do not appear to put athletes at greater risk for developing eating disorders. Certainly, any female athlete in these sports may be influenced by general societal pressures that promote thinness as an ideal and as a result might demonstrate an eating disturbance. But no evidence exists to indicate that any feature of these sports puts participants at higher risk than other women in our culture.

The possibility exists, however, that more sports will begin to demand thinness as a result of the continued emphasis on leaner bodies for athletes. For example, swimming has not traditionally been considered a thinness-demand sport in the same way that gymnastics, diving, distance running, and dancing have been. In recent years, however, swimmers have apparently felt a significant increase in pressure to lose weight and lower their body fat. And it now appears that the prevalence of eating disorders in swimmers may be higher.

Somehow we have to prevent this emphasis on thinness from being applied to other non-thinness-demand sports like basketball, softball, and volleyball. If the idea continues to grow that thinness makes a better athlete, at some point we may have no non-thinness-demand sports but more athletes with eating disorders.

Not that long ago, a controversy in women's sports involved *increased* size, strength, and athletic performance. In the 1976 Olympics and other international competitions, swimming, track and field, and other sports were frequently dominated by women from Eastern bloc countries. These women were often noticeably larger and apparently stronger than many women from Western countries like the United States. Western competitors and the Western media complained that these athletes were using steroids to increase their size and strength. Even though the complaints focused on steroid use, the implicit message was that the smaller Western women were forced to compete at an unfair disadvantage. Some people even wanted these athletes to undergo medical tests to determine if they were in fact women.

We seem to have moved a great distance in a short time. Today, we seldom see women competitors who look too big, too strong, or too masculine. Rather, we see smaller, leaner athletes who sometimes not only look like prepubescent girls but may actually be prepubescent girls. If more sports move in that direction, soon no sports at all may carry a low risk for eating disorders.

CHAPTER 4

Athletes With Eating Disorders

Research and treatment of eating disorders in athletes are still relatively undeveloped. Consequently, our state of knowledge, especially for male athletes, is not as extensive or as scientifically based as we would like. Much of what follows has been drawn from clinical case material, and to a lesser degree from anecdotal information from current and former athletes, many of whom have been in treatment for anorexia nervosa or bulimia nervosa. Although males with eating disorders are probably similar in many respects to their female counterparts, we'll discuss male athletes separately.

We'll also divide our discussion of athletes with eating disorders by disorder—anorexia nervosa, bulimia nervosa, and eating disorder NOS. This is not to imply that these disorders can be clearly distinguished from each other; this somewhat artificial division is primarily for instructional purposes. We've pointed out that eating disorders occur on a continuum, and athletes may move on the continuum, exhibiting different eating characteristics at various times during their athletic careers. So although we will be describing athletes with these "different" disorders, remember that they are usually more alike than different, regardless of diagnosis.

Athletes With Anorexia Nervosa

In many ways, athletes with anorexia will resemble other individuals with anorexia. They are noticeable by their overly thin appearance and their resistance to eating. They are apt to be perfectionistic while pursuing unrealistic goals, and much of their behavior is compulsive and ritualistic, especially with regard to eating and eating-related behaviors like weighing and exercise. Their thinking is typically absolute, concrete, and obsessive, particularly with respect to their weight and eating, and they complain about being or feeling fat despite being obviously underweight and even emaciated. Despite such irrational thoughts and unusual behaviors, individuals with anorexia seldom complain or express emotions openly or directly. When confronted with the disorder, they maintain that they are fine and have no problems.

Female Athletes With Anorexia Nervosa

Although similar to female anorexics who are not athletes, affected female athletes are also apt to be different in some ways; these differences can be seen primarily in the athletic realm.

CASE STUDY

Andrea

Andrea was a 25-year-old competitive cyclist who reluctantly reported that she had always been a good athlete and student. She initially presented for treatment with relationship problems. When asked in her initial session about her eating, she denied any difficulty, but she was quite thin and admitted having recently lost 10 pounds as a result of training. After about 6 weeks in treatment, Andrea's eating disorder became more apparent, for she had lost a noticeable amount of weight. When pressed, Andrea admitted that she was following a very restricted regimen of vegetables and grains, about 1,000 calories daily. (In actuality, she probably ate less than 600 calories a day.) Accuracy was difficult to determine because of her avoidance of the topic and her reticence in recording or even reporting her intake. She ate only at specific times, usually the same three or four foods each day. At the same time, she was training for hours each day, often riding more than 50 miles. When confronted about the discrepancy between her caloric intake and her energy expenditure, she remarked that her sport required endurance training and that she had plenty of energy. She also saw the exercise as a way to get rid of the "fat" on her "huge thighs." Andrea further claimed that she was not really losing weight, despite being informed that she was losing approximately a pound a week. At 5'7" tall and 104 pounds, she did not think she was too thin, especially for a cyclist. She and her coach both believed that a leaner cyclist could perform better. This was reinforced at cycling training camps, where she was used as a model for other cyclists. In the early stages of her disorder, Andrea performed well despite her disorder and used her performance to rationalize her eating and training regimens. As she developed overuse injuries and her performance began to deteriorate, she was unable to accept that her inadequate nutrition and excessive exercise were responsible. Rather, she believed that she could perform better if she just worked harder and continued to reduce her body fat. She reported that many of her competitors were thinner than she was, and some performed better. Andrea was very controlled in her therapy sessions and only very rarely showed any emotion. On these occasions, a few tears would slip through her defenses, only to be quickly wiped away. When her therapist commented on this minimal emotional expression, Andrea remarked that she did not know where the tears had come from; therefore, she must be fine. Additionally, even though her weight continued to decrease and her exercising became more out of her control, she still questioned whether she really had a problem.

Sport Environment.   As Andrea's story demonstrates, one of the primary differences between the nonathlete and the athlete with anorexia nervosa is that the athlete may use her sport to "legitimize" her disorder. The current emphasis on thinness in the sport environment as it relates to performance makes it easier for the athlete to rationalize her behavior as well as to "hide" within her sport. This is particularly true for sports that emphasize a thin shape or form in their scoring, and for sports that stress a thin shape, low body weight or low body fat levels for performance.

This emphasis on thinness in sports allows the athlete to believe that she is restricting her eating to do what she is supposed to do—increase or improve athletic performance and become a better athlete. By restricting her caloric (fat) intake, she believes she can lower her body fat; by exercising more, she can get into better shape. Also, the hyperactivity that often accompanies anorexia nervosa is consistent with her need to exercise; she believes that she has more than enough energy and feels better (actually less anxious) when she expends it. As a result of her dieting and exercising, she believes she will be quicker, faster, and stronger and will build greater cardiovascular endurance and therefore her performance will have to improve. If it doesn't, she will likely convince herself that she is not thin enough yet and attempt to lose even more weight. Even though an outsider would consider this thinking irrational given the athlete's anorexia, for her these beliefs are quite real and believable. She may have actually improved her performance previously when she began to reduce weight and body fat. In fact, some athletes with anorexia nervosa are enormously successful in their sport during the early stages of their disorder. Or she may have selectively perceived that the thinnest competitors in her sport usually perform better. Under these circumstances, it is very difficult to convince the athlete to give up her disorder or give up her sport to undergo treatment. These experiences usually serve only to induce further caloric restriction.

At some point, the performance of an athlete like Andrea inevitably declines due to the effects of malnutrition. However, rather than viewing low caloric intake as the problem and increased intake as a solution, she believes instead that she needs to be thinner to regain her previous competitive level. Basing her belief on her own experience, what coaches or other athletes have told her, or what she has read, she is convinced that thinner, leaner athletes perform better. If others confront her about an eating disorder, she may use her high level of sport performance to "prove" that she does not have an eating disorder, claiming that she could not perform as well as she does if she were sick.

Eating.   Anorexic individuals are adept at finding excuses for their infrequent or inadequate eating. The athlete with anorexia nervosa probably has more of these excuses than the nonathlete due to the nature and demands of the sport environment. She may claim that with all the demands of competition, training, practice, meetings, and traveling, she does not always have enough time to eat. Or she may never eat on road trips because "We always stop at fast-food places and I don't want to eat fatty junk food before a game." Perhaps she maintains that she cannot eat before practice or competition because she is too nervous, or that it makes her feel heavy or nauseated. By the same token, she may claim that eating shortly after the physical exertion of practice or competition makes her feel sick. Actual physical symptoms such as abdominal pain, bloating, and postprandial distress (discomfort after eating) are common complaints of individuals with anorexia nervosa (Mitchell, 1986), and experiencing them reinforces the belief that it is better not to eat before competition.

The athlete with anorexia nervosa, especially in thinness-demand sports, may attempt to justify her low weight and eating habits by reporting that other female athletes she knows are thinner than she is and eat less, yet they apparently have no difficulties and are performing well. Because athletes often wear revealing uniforms and frequently shower and change clothes together, it is easy for them to make unhelpful comparisons of body sizes, shapes, and weights. All these comparisons, combined with the anorexic's body-image distortion (seeing body parts or the entire body as larger than actual size), enable her to see what she needs to see to justify her need to be thin.

The affected athlete may claim that she cannot ingest dietary fat because she must lower her body fat composition to enhance performance, thereby rationalizing the elimination of several foods, most notably meat. She may become a vegetarian—or more accurately a "pseudo-vegetarian." The pseudo-vegetarian becomes a vegetarian after the onset of her disorder, and although she claims the change is motivated by her ethical or moral stance regarding the ingestion of animal products, her primary goal and concern is still to reduce dietary fat to lose weight. As a result, the pseudo-vegetarian athlete not only claims that her meatless regimen is to improve performance, but that it also conforms to her value system. And she may extend it to include all animal products, such as dairy foods and eggs.

Use of Exercise. The athlete with anorexia nervosa, like the nonathlete, is apt to exercise excessively, compulsively, and as a form of purgation. She may feel anxious, guilty, depressed, and "fat" when unable to exercise, as do nonathletes. However, the athlete also believes she is losing a significant part of her identity when she is not able or allowed to train and compete.

The athlete with anorexia is also driven to exercise and compete by her need to please (or her fear of displeasing) significant others (i.e., her coaches, parents, teammates) because she believes (has been taught) that an athlete cannot work too hard—that a serious, committed athlete "plays with pain." Consequently, her fear, anxiety, perfectionism, and high need for achievement help push her to exercise when she is sick or injured. She may claim that if she reduces her exercise or practice, she may lose playing time or her position on the team and gain weight that would hurt her performance. In reality, she is attempting to avoid the anxiety, fear, depression, or guilt she feels when she does not exercise. As a result, she finds it difficult to taper her exercise during her competitive season and to take time off or even reduce her training in the off-season. Finally, when she is told she must curtail or eliminate her exercise due to the disorder, the athlete will respond with the same negative feelings as the nonathlete, as well as other feelings that are unique to her role and identity as an athlete.

Interestingly, as important as exercise typically is to an individual with anorexia nervosa, the athlete with anorexia may refuse to lift weights as part of her sport training. She may feel that weight training, especially work on the lower body, will add too much muscle. Although most athletes approve of adding lean muscle mass, some with anorexia fear that it will add weight because "muscle is heavy."

Denial and Rationalization. The anorexic individual's ability to deny her disorder and rationalize her thoughts and behaviors can be quite sophisticated and can even extend to her physical symptoms. For example, one anorexic athlete explained that her bradycardia (slow heart rate) and hypotension (low blood pressure) occurred simply because she had an "athlete's heart." Another athlete attributed her exercise-induced chest pain to the fact that her cardiovascular health had been compromised because she had not been allowed to exercise while she spent two days in the hospital the previous week.

Many of the anorexic individual's gastrointestinal symptoms mentioned previously—abdominal pain, bloating, nausea, cramps, diarrhea, and constipation—are common complaints of many serious runners as well (Mangi, Jokl, & Dayton, 1979). The sophisticated distance runner with anorexia nervosa can claim that her symptoms are due to her running rather than to her disorder. She might further rationalize that using laxatives and diuretics is simply her way of dealing with the digestive problems associated with being a runner.

In a similar vein, the amenorrheic athlete with anorexia nervosa may claim that she does not want menstruation to return because it makes her feel bloated and heavy or interferes with training. Further, she usually knows many successful female athletes who have no menstrual cycles, and they seem to be doing well. She may use this information to support her claim that her amenorrhea results from her being an athlete rather than being anorexic.

Injury. In all likelihood, an athlete with anorexia nervosa will have injuries that interfere with sport performance and also create difficulties with exercise and training. The way she handles injuries is characteristic of many obligatory or compulsive exercisers. Denial and rationalization are common. In the likely event that she is injured, she is apt to try to "run through the pain" rather than resting and recuperating until her injury heals. She may ignore the advice of physicians, trainers, and coaches and exercise anyway, or at least overdo what they have recommended for her. She may rationalize her noncompliance by saying that she knows her body better than anyone else does, when in actuality a variety of factors are pushing her to exercise despite painful injury. When the athlete's injuries or illnesses are simply too severe to allow her to exercise at all, she will tend to be even more restrictive about her caloric intake and again use her sport and sport performance as the rationale.

Identity. The nonathlete with anorexia nervosa needs to be thin. Often she cannot be specific about how thinness will benefit her, but she is nonetheless convinced that it will make her happier. The athlete has this same general need but also strives to be thin to realize her athletic goals. Her athletic performance helps her define who she is; part of her identity is that of an athlete. Unfortunately, it may be the only part of her identity that gives her even minimal self-esteem. As a result, threats to this identity can create considerable distress.

Most anorexic individuals question their worth; they fear that they have little value. They believe they must perform well at whatever they do to gain acceptance and approval. The athlete with anorexia is no different except that her achievements in sport afford her a small amount of self-esteem or good feeling. This in part motivates her to train and compete hard despite her fatigue, illness, or injury; she may feel that she has no choice. As one athlete put it when her coach benched her due to the effects of her disorder: "All I am is an anorexic ballplayer. Now, without playing, I'm just an anorexic!"

As we mentioned earlier, the good feeling an anorexic athlete may have about her performance tends to be minimal as well as fleeting. This is particularly true when she is participating in her sport not because she enjoys it, but because she is driven to do so by her irrational fear of becoming obese as well as her need to please significant others in her life. Under these circumstances, she seldom finds joy, excitement, or happiness in her sport achievements, regardless of how significant they might be. The athlete with anorexia who is successful even to the point of attaining elite status is likely to respond to her success not with joy or satisfaction but with added pressure—pressure to continue performing at that high level. At the same time, when sport performance diminishes, the psychological effect can be significant. Thus, sport performance for her becomes a competition that she cannot win. At worst, her performance will decline. At best, she continues to maintain her high-pressured level of performance.

The issue of identity is probably most significant for those individuals who have seriously trained for a sport or activity since early childhood. We can easily imagine how a 13-year-old gymnast who is rapidly approaching elite status or an 18-year-old ballet dancer who has completed her training in a prestigious ballet school might feel if her identity of gymnast or ballet dancer was threatened. The young gymnast may have begun her training at age 5. She may have given up many normal childhood activities to train. She may even have left her family to live at or near an exclusive training center. The ballet dancer may have begun her life as a dancer at age 7 or 8; she may have completed the preparation for her life's work at 18 and expected to be at the peak of her career at 21. These individuals may have little concept of themselves other than as a gymnast or a dancer; this is who they are. If they are anorexic, they may feel they have little else to offer. Consequently, any threat to their performance also threatens a fragile, one-dimensional identity.

Strengths.   Even though she is at a great deal of risk, the athlete with anorexia may in some ways be physically and emotionally stronger than the anorexic who is not an athlete. She is used to making sacrifices for her sport and not focusing on her aches and pains. She has learned to be mentally tougher and has been expected to perform despite adversity. As a result, she can probably persist longer before finally giving in to the complications of her disorder. Although this toughness perhaps puts her more at risk for developing a serious disorder before the problem is identified, it also appears to serve her well in treatment. Most important, it helps her respond to treatment with a toughness and persistence that allow her to take the risks necessary for getting over her disorder (i.e., increasing caloric intake despite her inevitable fears and anxieties that accompany it).

Non-Thinness-Demand Sports

We should not infer from the previous discussion that anorexia nervosa occurs only in athletes participating in sports that directly emphasize thinness. It can and does occur in athletes in all sports. An example comes from basketball, a sport that typically does not emphasize a small size or shape.

CASE STUDY

Barbara

Barbara was a 19-year-old college basketball player. There was no pressure from her coaches to be thin; in fact, they pressured her to gain weight. She had become so thin that she no longer had the strength or stamina to compete. Her coach had benched her until she gained enough weight to be competitive again. As much as Barbara wanted to return to basketball, she was nonetheless intensely afraid of gaining weight. The extent of her weight concerns was displayed in a ritual she practiced each time she was weighed during treatment. She would remove all of her clothing down to very thin shorts and a shirt. Finally, she would remove her jewelry, including a tiny crucifix. She very much needed to weigh as little as she possibly could, despite wanting to get well. Even though she knew the articles she removed before weighing did not constitute real body weight, she still needed to see "low numbers" on the scale. Her confict between wanting to play basketball to please her significant others and her fear of gaining weight was evidenced by her reaction whenever she saw her weight; although she tried not to show any emotion, she cried, regardless of what the scale read. If her weight was up, she was afraid she was getting fat. If her weight was not up, she was frustrated and fearful that not being able to play basketball would displease her coaches and parents.

Male Athletes With Anorexia Nervosa

Although the prevalence of anorexia nervosa is significantly lower in male athletes than in female athletes and appears to be low in males in the general population, Crisp and Burns (1990) suggested that sports may help mask anorexia in males and that anorexia may go undetected in male athletes and joggers. Thus, as we suggested earlier, eating disorders in male athletes may be underreported and underidentified. Part of the difficulty in this regard may be related to the cultural bias of viewing eating disorders as a "woman's problem." This bias makes it easier for the male to go unnoticed; the male anorexic is more apt to be seen as "very skinny," whereas the female is viewed as being "anorexic." For this reason, the male anorexic's difficulties may go undetected for a longer time, putting him at greater risk.

In general, anorexia nervosa as it occurs in males appears to be more similar than dissimilar to anorexia in females (Woodside, Garner, Rockert, & Garfinkel, 1990). We can only assume that these similarities hold true for athletes with eating disorders as well. At the same time, some important distinctions appear to exist. Most important, although males probably have similar predisposing factors, their reasons for dieting sometimes differ from women's. Andersen (1990) reports that the majority of males with anorexia have actually *been* overweight or obese before their eating disorder, whereas more women simply *felt* themselves to have been overweight. Consequently, the anorexic male athlete's desire to lose weight more often has a real-world basis. Thus, his fear of being overweight is less irrational than that of the female anorexic, who often has not been overweight. Andersen also reports that male anorexics tend to be less concerned about numbers of pounds or clothes sizes than their female counterparts. Additionally, although many diet in an effort to enhance sport performance and may be induced to diet by a coach, male anorexics also diet to make weight or to lose the weight they may have gained as a result of injury (Andersen, 1988, 1990).

Another difference between males and females with eating disorders that is relevant to athletes concerns the means by which they pursue weight loss. In general, males are probably more inclined to use exercise or other active means in an effort to lose weight (Drewnowski & Yee, 1987). Females may more often resort to more passive methods such as restrictive dieting or pathogenic weight loss practices such as vomiting, laxative abuse, or diuretic use (Black & Burckes-Miller, 1988). The reason for this is probably that dieting is simply more widely accepted for women than for men. Additionally, studies that have looked at body image and self-concept have found that males emphasize physical effectiveness rather than physical attractiveness (Lerner & Karabenick, 1974; Lerner, Orlos, & Knapp, 1976). For these reasons, the anorexic male athlete is probably more likely than the female to rationalize weight loss as a way to enhance sport performance rather than to improve appearance.

As we reported in chapter 3, male athlete groups most often affected are those that emphasize weight, such as wrestlers, distance runners, and jockeys. As with females, however, male athletes with anorexia nervosa are not found only in sports that emphasize low weight. They can also be found in sports that stress increased body size and weight, as in the following case study.

CASE STUDY

Bob

As a college football player, Bob had been small. At his coaches' urging, he had sought to increase his weight to become more competitive. Although his coaches had requested that he add any type of weight, Bob had focused on increasing his muscle mass. He became quite obsessive about not eating "high-fat" foods. The weight training he had been introduced to through football became compulsive and obligatory. Three years after he had completed his football eligibility, Bob sought treatment not for his eating disorder but because of difficulties with his girlfriend. She complained that he never had any time or energy for her due to his heavy training schedule. He believed that "she just didn't understand." Even though he was no longer in competitive sports, he was spending more time "staying in shape" than he ever had when he was playing football. When asked about this, he remarked that because he was not practicing football every day, he needed to exercise and "eat right" so he wouldn't "get fat." Bob did not view his restrictive no-fat regimen as a diet. Rather, he was concerned that the muscle he had added while playing football would "turn to fat" if he decreased his exercise and activity. When asked about his weight history, he stated that he had been overweight as a child before he "became serious about football." He said his weight was "around 140," although he refused to be weighed. At 5'10" tall, he was quite thin, especially considering that he had played football in college at "about 180."

Identifying Athletes With Anorexia Nervosa

Many, perhaps even most, individuals with anorexia nervosa do not believe they have a problem and therefore do not usually seek treatment on their own. For this reason, identification of these individuals is extremely important if they are to receive the treatment they need as soon as is reasonably possible. Physical and psychological characteristics may indicate the presence of anorexia nervosa in an athlete. However, remember that the presence of some of these characteristics does not mean that an individual is anorexic. At the same time, the likelihood of the disorder being present increases with the number of characteristics that a particular individual displays.

Physical Symptoms of Athletes With Anorexia Nervosa

1. Amenorrhea
2. Dehydration, especially in the absence of training or competition
3. Fatigue beyond that normally expected in training or competition

4. Gastrointestinal problems (i.e., constipation, diarrhea, bloating, postprandial distress)
5. Hyperactivity
6. Hypothermia (cold intolerance)
7. Lanugo (fine hair on face and arms)
8. Muscle weakness
9. Overuse injuries
10. Significant weight loss beyond that necessary for adequate sport performance
11. Stress fractures
12. Weight significantly lower than necessary for adequate sport performance

Psychological and Behavioral Characteristics of Athletes With Anorexia Nervosa

1. Anxiety, both related and unrelated to sport performance
2. Avoidance of eating and eating situations
3. Claims of "feeling fat" despite being thin
4. Compulsiveness and rigidity, especially regarding eating and exercise
5. Depression
6. Excessive or obligatory exercise beyond that required for a particular sport or coach
7. Exercising while injured despite prohibitions by medical and training staffs
8. Insomnia
9. Obsessiveness and preoccupation with weight and eating while being at a low weight and engaging in minimal eating
10. Resistance to weight gain or maintenance recommended by sport support staff
11. Restlessness—relaxing is difficult or impossible
12. Restrictive dieting, especially when self-imposed and unnecessary for, or detrimental to, sport performance
13. Social withdrawal from teammates and sport support staff, as well as from people outside sports
14. Unusual weighing behavior (i.e., excessive weighing, refusal to weigh, negative reaction to being weighed)

Effects of Anorexia Nervosa on Sport Performance

Anorexia nervosa can negatively affect sport performance as a consequence of both its physiological and psychological complications. These negative effects are apt to vary among athletes for several reasons. Most important, the magnitude of the effect is related to the severity and chronicity of the disorder. Also, the effects can relate generally to the athlete's overall health, or they can be specific to particular body systems. The effects of the disorder can vary depending on individual differences in the athlete's family history, body constitution, and health status before the disorder. Finally, the effects on performance can vary depending on the physical demands of particular sports. For example, anorexia nervosa will probably have different effects on an endurance athlete such as a distance runner than on an athlete in a less aerobic sport or in an anaerobic sport such as diving.

Physiological

The physiological complications of anorexia nervosa are numerous, and any one of them can negatively affect performance. One of the most important involves the depletion of muscle glycogen stores. Under normal circumstances, intensive or excessive exercise requires glucose as an energy source; this glucose is replenished and stored as glycogen during nonexercise periods through the ingestion of carbohydrates. If the athlete exercises excessively, as many with anorexia do, the need for glucose or glycogen increases, yet the body has less time or opportunity to replenish and store glycogen. Fearing that ingesting carbohydrates will result in weight gain, many athletes with anorexia nervosa avoid them. As a result, the athlete's body is not able to store necessary glycogen. As training continues, fatigue and its inevitable effects on performance must at some point occur.

The athlete with anorexia nervosa is apt to suffer losses in muscular strength, endurance, speed, and coordination. At least some of these losses can be attributed to dehydration. In fact, a 1% loss of body fluid can greatly decrease exercise performance (Mangi et al., 1979). As the athlete loses more fluid, performance will likely decrease more. Bergstrom and Hultman (1972) reported that a fluid loss of 5% of the athlete's body weight can result in a 20% to 30% decrease in muscular work capacity. In addition, aerobic power will likely decrease, as will oxygen utilization. The heart and circulatory system can be significantly affected, with difficulties sometimes being reflected in reduced blood volume and heart function. Relatedly, starvation associated with anorexia nervosa can reduce cardiac chamber dimensions and left ventricle mass, resulting in reduced working capacity during exercise (Stephenson, 1991).

Skeletal system problems can negatively affect sport performance in women athletes with anorexia nervosa or even prohibit it altogether. The combination of amenorrhea and low body weight that is characteristic of anorexia nervosa appears to place the female athlete at greater risk for skeletal injuries such as stress fractures. More specifically, the work of Drinkwater and her associates (Drinkwater, Bruemner, & Chesnut, 1990; Drinkwater et al., 1984) suggests an interaction between menstrual pattern, body weight, and vertebral density. Vertebral density decreases with the severity of menstrual irregularity, and body weight becomes a more critical factor in vertebral density loss as menstrual irregularity becomes more severe. This suggests that the low-weight athlete who has been amenorrheic for an extended period is at a higher risk for stress fractures. These findings have been corroborated by studies reporting higher incidences of stress fractures in amenorrheic athletes (Barrow & Sha, 1988; Clark et al., 1988; Marcus et al., 1985) and bone injuries and fractures in amenorrheic ballet dancers (Benson, Geiger, Eiserman, & Wardlaw, 1989; Warren, Brooks-Gunn, Hamilton, Warren, & Hamilton, 1986) than in their normally menstruating counterparts.

Psychological

Although athletes with anorexia nervosa can sometimes perform at high levels for extended periods, the athlete's physical condition nonetheless places a ceiling on what the athlete's body is able to accomplish. The athlete's psychological makeup then determines how close to that ceiling she is able to perform. Up to a point, she is able to use her psychological component in many ways to override the disorder's medical or physical effects. Despite her psychological efforts, however, the medical complications associated with the disorder will at some point lower that ceiling. Eventually, the psychological part of the individual also succumbs to the disorder, no longer able to offset the physical complications. The psychological component may then begin to actively contribute to poorer performance.

Psychologically, the anorexic athlete's performance can be negatively affected in part because she often experiences agitation, anxiety, and fear. Probably a greater contributor is depression. Depression can significantly affect all aspects of the individual's performance. Physically, it can slow and weaken the athlete. It can also affect the athlete's energy and activity levels. Emotionally, the depressed athlete is apt to feel "down," "flat," helpless, or hopeless. Mentally, thinking may be slower and more negative. Concentration becomes more difficult, due not only to depression but also to other psychological and nutritional factors. From a psychological point of view, excessive restriction of caloric intake tends to make the individual obsessive about eating, food, weight, and her body, thereby reducing concentration on other things. From a nutritional standpoint, the brain needs adequate nutrition, especially complex carbohydrates, to function properly. Finally, for a variety of reasons, the athlete with anorexia often has trouble sleeping, or difficulty falling asleep. If the individual's depression is severe enough, sleep may be disturbed by early-morning waking. Insomnia or sleep difficulty is likely to contribute to fatigue, irritability, and poor concentration.

The combination of poor nutrition, fatigue, negative emotions, poor concentration, and sleep difficulty is apt to interfere with optimal performance. The athlete with anorexia nervosa is less often able to use emotion to get "psyched up" for competition. With concentration impaired, she may make more mental mistakes, use poorer judgment, and think more negatively. Her depression, in addition to being responsible in part for these difficulties, can also result in psychomotor retardation, slowing her down mentally as well as physically.

Success Despite Disorder

Even with the difficult and sometimes serious physiological and psychological effects of anorexia, some athletes are still able to exercise and participate in their sports. In many cases, they even perform at high levels. Their bodies can apparently continue exercising despite being malnourished, unhealthy, and tired. Although physically and emotionally exhausted, they are sometimes able to motivate themselves enough to perform long after others would have stopped. Given the physical and emotional state of athletes with anorexia nervosa, their persistence and in some cases high levels of performance seems improbable if not impossible. How can they continue to perform as well as they do for so long?

Anorexia nervosa is a very complex disorder, which in part explains the complexity of the answer to this question. Both psychological/behavioral and physiological aspects or characteristics of the individual are involved.

Psychological/Behavioral. Interestingly, many of the characteristics that put an individual at risk for developing anorexia nervosa also make it possible for him or her to function under very difficult circumstances. Individuals with anorexia are often driven by fear, anxiety, and guilt. These feelings can drive them even when they are exhausted. Compulsive rituals and never-ending activity distract anorexics from depression, anxiety, and fatigue. Additionally, they are often afraid to curtail or stop their activity; doing so makes them feel too uncomfortable. Any behavior that helps an individual avoid fear and anxiety can very quickly become reinforced, and the individual can begin to experience the behavior as pleasurable. To a person with anorexia nervosa, exercising when she's tired and sick may feel better than not exercising.

Not only are anorexic individuals usually afraid to stop their activity or exercise, many believe that they cannot stop. The hyperactivity that frequently accompanies the disorder makes it difficult for them to stop. The compulsive personality many anorexics exhibit makes it difficult for them to change their routines, regardless of how tired they are. Even if they could stop without feeling anxious or afraid, many would probably feel guilty. Finally, their ability to deny and distort how they are feeling is usually quite sophisticated. This is why they often appear to be unaffected by feelings and sensations that would significantly and negatively affect other people.

These characteristics explain in part how the individual can persist despite her disorder. Another explanation for the success of some anorexic athletes is again related to the characteristics that put them at risk for the disorder. Very few people work harder than people with anorexia. Because of their low self-esteem and perfectionism, they are seldom if ever satisfied with their performance or themselves; in essence, they never feel "good enough." A strong need for approval (or fear of disapproval) and a related need to please others can drive them. They are willing to deprive and push themselves even when exhausted. They can tolerate pain and discomfort.

We believe that anorexic individuals in many ways are very strong people. In fact, a person probably cannot be anorexic without being strong. Not very many people can deprive themselves of food and push themselves like the anorexic can. Although anorexics often use these strengths in ways that may cause themselves physical and mental harm, these same strengths probably help the athlete with anorexia nervosa achieve success despite the disorder. This does not mean that the athlete is successful because she is anorexic; rather, the anorexic athlete can use the "strengths" or characteristics necessary to be anorexic—the ability to deny physical and emotional discomfort, a high need for achievement (perfectionism) and approval, persistence, and a willingness to overwork—to be successful in athletics.

Physiological. The anorexic's ability to push herself despite her difficulties may have a physiological basis for some athletes. As discussed earlier (p. 27), Epling and his associates proposed a bio-behavioral theory regarding the relationship between excessive exercise and reduced food intake. They suggested that excessive exercise leads to a decrease in eating that in turn leads to more exercise.

Often, the anorexic's activity is drug-induced; that is, the body may be running on drug effects in lieu of energy provided through caloric intake. Many anorexic individuals use diet pills, or they may ingest large quantities of caffeine in the form of coffee, tea, and caffeinated diet soft drinks. They may take other stimulants in an effort to stay awake to get more done each day. This drug effect may be strong enough to override the effects of malnutrition and fatigue, especially in the earlier stages of the disorder.

Athletes With Bulimia Nervosa

In many respects, athletes with bulimia nervosa are like their nonathlete counterparts. Similarities include that it is difficult to discern that they have a problem simply by looking at them. They may be underweight, but typically not as underweight as the anorexic. More often they are within normal weight ranges. They may also be overweight. Their eating is apt to vary; an individual may consume very little or nothing at all on one occasion and eat large volumes of food on others. Similarly, their moods and emotions tend to be variable and unstable, ranging from normal to very depressed. Self-esteem is likely quite low, with self-dissatisfaction being voiced frequently. Many bulimic individuals show a low tolerance for frustration and anxiety; their behavior is often impulsive or irresponsible. They are apt to be obsessed with body size and shape, to see themselves as larger than they are, and to show a willingness to try almost any weight loss regimen.

Female Athletes With Bulimia Nervosa

Although athletes with bulimia nervosa are similar to nonathletes, some differences exist that relate to the athletic environment, as with the anorexic athlete.

CASE STUDY

Tammy

Tammy was an attractive collegiate gymnast who sought treatment because she was having difficulty getting along with her coach. This difficulty was actually a side effect or complication of her bulimia. At 5'0" tall and 92 pounds, she believed that she was "close to being too big to be a gymnast." For this reason, she tried "not to eat" all day, hoping that she could then "go to bed and sleep" so she would not have to eat. Her bulimia reinforced her belief that she could not eat normally. On some occasions, she could go without eating for two or three days. Then, however, she would become so hungry that she would begin to eat and then not be able to stop until she had eaten too much (binged). Tammy would then tell herself that she "had blown it" and that "I might as well eat all I want because I'm going to throw it up anyway." On "bad days," as she referred to them, she might consume more than 5,000 calories throughout the day and vomit a minimum of five times. She believed that if she did not "get rid of the food," not only would she become "fat," but she would not be able to perform well as a gymnast. Tammy's difficulty with her coach was not the cause of her bulimia. Her coach was not even aware of her disorder. Tammy was unsure about her gymnastic ability. At the same time, she believed she had little else to offer. Her uncertainty or "fear of not being good enough" combined with her fasting-induced hunger made it virtually impossible for her to resist binge eating and purging. Her bingeing and purging often occurred just before practice. As a result, she frequently felt too sick and weak to attend practices and used this excuse to avoid them. Tammy did not realize that missing practice also protected her from confronting her fear of inadequacy as a gymnast. Her coach thought she was missing practice too frequently, even with her excuse of sickness, and began to believe that Tammy was an "irresponsible malingerer." Tammy did not feel that she could tell her coach about her bulimia. As fearful as she was about her ability as a gymnast, she was even more afraid that the coach might not allow her to continue with the team. Tammy was also afraid that her coach might contact Tammy's parents, who did not know about her bulimia.

Eating.   Whereas an anorexic athlete's eating is very restricted, rigidly controlled, and predictable, the bulimic athlete's eating is apt to be quite variable and erratic. Like Tammy, she may eat very little if at all on some occasions. She will most likely use many of the same rationalizations her anorexic counterpart uses regarding not eating. Similarly, her role as an athlete allows her to use enhancement of sport performance to legitimize her dieting and to be thinner than is necessary. However, the athlete with bulimia nervosa also has another reason for not eating. Whereas the anorexic individual usually has only *fears* that her eating will get out of control, the person with bulimia has actual *experiences*—her bingeing—that confirm for her that she can lose control when she eats. In essence, her fears associated with eating are less irrational. Consequently, she may rationalize not eating by telling herself that she would rather not eat than run the risk of overeating (and purging).

Although the bulimic athlete's eating can take many forms, some tendencies appear to emerge. One involves Tammy's strategy of trying not to eat all day but bingeing in the evening. Even though this pattern is not different from that of many nonathlete bulimics, the rationale for not eating may be different. Many of the bulimic athlete's rationalizations for not eating all day are similar, even identical, to those of the anorexic athlete. For example, if she has a morning workout, such as a swim or run, she may claim that eating breakfast will make her feel too heavy. If she has an afternoon workout, she may say she cannot eat breakfast or lunch before exercising.

For the athlete with bulimia nervosa, skipping meals means there may be long periods between times that she eats. By the end of the day, she may not have eaten anything while she has practiced strenuously. Obviously, in this situation the bulimic athlete is apt to be extremely hungry.

Extreme hunger increases the likelihood that the individual will binge eat. Even if she does not intend to do so, she may find it very difficult to control her eating due to her intense hunger. Such was the case for Tammy, but the story of a distance runner probably provides a clearer example. This particular athlete tried not to eat during the day. As we might expect, she was extremely hungry by the end of the day. Because she did not keep food at her apartment for fear that she would eat it, she would go to the grocery store at these times intending to buy nutritious food to take home and prepare. As she tried to shop, however, her hunger caused her to be distracted by the candy displays. As a result, she would begin to snack right in the store. Often she would not stop until she had consumed 2 or 3 pounds of chocolate. Feeling that she had eaten too much, she would leave the grocery store without food. She would usually purge through vomiting. The next day, she would force herself to exercise enough to compensate for what she had eaten; in addition, she would again fast all day, thus restarting her cycle of exercising without eating, which would again eventually lead to binge eating.

The precipitants for the bulimic's binge eating were discussed in chapter 1. As with the distance runner just discussed, bingeing may be a purely physiological, hunger-related response to caloric restriction (Polivy & Herman, 1985). However, binge eating may have other precipitants as well. For the athlete with bulimia, these may or may not be related to sport. We must remember that the bulimic individual uses bingeing and purging to manage difficult emotions such as depression or anxiety. Consequently, bingeing and purging may be related to aspects of the athlete's life that have little or nothing to do with sport.

Although binge eating is often precipitated by dieting, it can also be a response to emotionality. This may or may not be directly related to the athlete's sport. In Tammy's case, her bingeing was related to her fear and anxiety about performing well enough as a gymnast. In actuality, it was also probably related to her general sense of inadequacy. Tammy used bingeing to avoid having to perform. Another athlete might be so anxious about competition that she may binge and purge before competing in an effort to deal with her anxiety. On the other hand, an athlete's reasons for bingeing and purging may have more to do with significant life issues than with competition itself. For example, one athlete with bulimia binged and purged before competition only when her parents were in attendance. From experience, she knew that bingeing and purging just before competition could negatively affect her performance. She was very afraid of displeasing her parents, not only in her sport performance but in all aspects of her life. Consequently, when her parents attended her competitions, her anxiety heightened to the point that she needed to binge and purge for "relief."

Obviously, sport can play a major or minor role in the athlete's bingeing and purging. The following case of a collegiate swimmer provides an excellent example of how an athlete's bingeing and purging can relate to issues both within and outside her athletic world.

CASE STUDY

Robin

When Robin presented for treatment at age 21, she had had her disorder for approximately 4 years. She reported a series of events that she believed had contributed to the development of her bulimia. First, she had experienced a knee injury that significantly curtailed her training. Second, her parents' usually difficult relationship had worsened, resulting in their separation. These events were essentially out of her control and had left her feeling helpless. Robin had also recently broken off a relationship with her boyfriend, which added to her difficulties. Fearing that her problems might create more turmoil for her parents, she kept her feelings and concerns to herself. This combination of events led her to binge eat in an effort to deal with the helplessness and depression she felt. Binge eating and significantly reduced exercise resulted in weight gain. When she returned to training and competition, her performance was less than it had been before her injury. She, her coach, and others attributed this decrease in performance, correctly or incorrectly, to increased weight. Her attempts to lose weight through dieting resulted in more binge eating. Shortly thereafter, she began vomiting in an attempt to regain her previous weight and competitive level.

Eating in the Team Environment. As difficult as eating is for the anorexic athlete while traveling with a team, it is perhaps even more difficult for the athlete with bulimia nervosa. The anorexic's eating (or lack thereof) becomes noticeable because she is so thin, but the bulimic's eating is often noticeable because she stays so thin despite sometimes eating large quantities of food. The bulimic athlete fears that her eating will get out of control while she's with other team members, and she will be embarrassed. She also wonders what she will do if she needs to purge. She worries that others will detect her bulimia and fears that her eating disorder will displease people and cause them to reject her. For this reason, she feels she cannot possibly risk detection.

The athlete with bulimia nervosa traveling with her team faces a dilemma. She does not believe that she can eat without bingeing. Consequently, she sees two difficult options: She will eat and try to be discrete about bingeing and purging, or she will avoid eating. The problems inherent in the first option are obvious, but the second option also has its difficulties. First, not eating is also apt to draw attention to her eating problem. Second, trying not to eat often leads to bingeing and purging. And third, if she is able to not eat, she may not have enough energy to perform at a satisfactory level. Obviously, this dilemma can cause even more worries for the athlete with bulimia. In fact, while traveling with teammates, some of these athletes worry more about their eating and being "found out" than about the upcoming competition.

This already difficult situation is exacerbated by the fact that athletes, especially those in thinness-demand sports, tend to be very

focused on eating. In particular, they are likely to watch how the thinnest and most successful of their teammates are eating. Being watched by other people usually creates more anxiety and pressure for the bulimic individual, which unfortunately she often manages through bingeing and purging. Even if others are not watching, the bulimic person may believe they are; she assumes that because she is watching herself and her teammates eat, everyone else must be doing the same. Obviously, with all her fears and worries associated with eating, the bulimic athlete's concentration and subsequent sport performance are likely to suffer.

Another difficult eating situation for the athlete with bulimia nervosa involves "carbohydrate loading." Coaches sometimes recommend the strategy of storing glycogen through eating lots of carbohydrates, especially for athletes who will be exerting excessive energy for an extended period, such as in distance running. Unfortunately, however, for many bulimic athletes this practice is too similar to binge eating. Due to their dieting, they may already crave carbohydrates. Carbohydrates may also be the type of food they typically binge on. When the athlete with bulimia nervosa attempts to load carbohydrates, he or she is apt to start binge eating, which may be followed by purging. What the bulimic athlete begins as an attempt to store energy for later use in strenuous competition can result in her feeling physically drained and dehydrated as a result of purging. Interestingly, however, the bulimic athlete may also use carbohydrate loading to rationalize her binge eating. Given these potential problems for the athlete with bulimia nervosa, as well as questions regarding the effectiveness and safety of carbohydrate loading in general, we do not recommend its use with athletes who are actively bulimic or who are recovering from the disorder.

Although the anorexic individual is not often convinced that she has an eating problem, the person who is bingeing and purging knows that her eating is abnormal. Nonetheless, when evaluating how much she eats, the bulimic is often as inaccurate as the anorexic. In addition to overestimating how much she eats and its caloric value, the bulimic individual often considers the bingeing that she does before purging as eating. So when asked if she has eaten, she will say yes. This was true for a swimmer who was bingeing and purging three or four times daily while participating in a sport that required considerable energy output on a regular basis. In fact, the only nutrition she received came from whatever food remained in her body after purging. However, even after she had begun treatment, she still considered herself to have eaten following a binge-purge episode.

Another athlete illustrates a very different relationship between sport performance and eating. This particular young woman allowed herself to eat healthy foods in reasonable amounts only on the day of a competition. It seemed as if she knew that she needed good nutrition to perform well, and if she was competing, she could rationalize allowing herself to eat. Unfortunately, competition was the only rationale she could (or would) use for eating in a healthy manner. Of course, after the competition she not only went back to her bulimic cycle of dieting and bingeing but was even more restrictive with dieting to compensate for the eating she had done.

Exercise.   Although athletes with bulimia are in many ways similar to bulimic individuals who are not athletes, they are also different in many respects. Part of this difference involves exercise. Obviously, exercise is a significant part of the bulimic athlete's life. Many nonathlete bulimics do not exercise at all, much less excessively. For those who do, it is much easier to determine when their exercise is excessive and when they are using it as a form of purging. Because many sports demand very high levels of exercise, it is more difficult to determine how bulimic athletes are using their exercise. They may be using it as a means to lose weight, regardless of whether the weight loss is designed to improve appearance or enhance sport performance. They may be using it as a form of purging, to undo the effects of eating. It may be a compulsive behavior designed to help them deal with fear and anxiety. Finally, an athlete may use exercise to punish herself; one patient forced herself to run 6 to 8 miles after bingeing—not because she was attempting to undo the effects of eating, but to punish herself for being "bad."

Exercise often plays a somewhat different role for the bulimic athlete than for the anorexic athlete. The bulimic is usually able to be less compulsive about exercise. Whereas the anorexic athlete will not miss an opportunity to exercise, the bulimic athlete may create an opportunity to miss it, depending on how she is feeling. Tammy, the gymnast who was not performing well in practice (primarily due to difficulties associated with her disorder), provides an example. In an effort to deal with her anxiety about poor sport performance, she would often binge and purge before practice. Even though she was unaware of it, she was using her bulimia to make her feel bad enough physically that she could ask her coach to excuse her from practice. If the coach refused, she could blame her poor performance during practice on not feeling well. Interestingly, she would often binge and purge even when the coach did excuse her, because she felt bad about missing practice.

Responsibility Issues.   Not only is the athlete with bulimia sometimes willing to miss practice, she can also be quite irresponsible about practice—she may be late or may not show up at all. This irresponsibility, or what appears to be irresponsibility, may be related to her sport as in the previous example, or it may be related to any number of other issues or difficulties she may be experiencing. In any event, this irresponsible behavior obviously sets her apart from the rigid adherence to rules and responsibilities of her anorexic counterpart. However, it also indicates the variability of mood, attitude, and behavior characteristic of the bulimic. Although this individual can be quite irresponsible on occasion, she can also be overly compliant and cooperative, very coachable, and intensely loyal to her team and coach.

Body Dissatisfaction.   Another difference between the bulimic athlete and the bulimic nonathlete involves body dissatisfaction. Bulimics, whether athletes or not, want to be thin, just as anorexics do. Many bulimics also experience body image distortion like anorexics, although not usually to the same extent. However, being thin is not enough for the bulimic. Whereas the anorexic is typically characterized by a relentless pursuit of thinness, the bulimic seeks not only thinness but often the perfect shape or form through thinness. Both athlete and nonathlete bulimics express body dissatisfaction with either specific body parts or the entire body. However, athletes in general tend to be less dissatisfied with their bodies than their nonathlete counterparts, and we assume this is also true when bulimic athletes are compared to bulimics who are not athletes. Exceptions exist, of course, perhaps more often in sports that emphasize thinness or a small shape or in sports such as swimming or diving in which the body is exposed.

Male Athletes with Bulimia Nervosa

It appears that males and females with bulimia are not radically different. Thus, we assume that male athletes with the disorder are similar to their female counterparts. As with anorexia nervosa, the primary difference is that they may be dieting for different reasons, which we discussed previously. Males with eating disorders tend to diet in response to advice from a coach, to prevent or decrease weight gain following an injury, and to make wrestling weight (Andersen, 1988). The following case of a wrestler is illustrative.

CASE STUDY

Mark

When he sought treatment, Mark reported that he had been bulimic since early in his high school wrestling career. He had no doubt that the demand to "make weight" for wrestling was the precipitating factor in his disorder. Before his involvement in wrestling, he had had no concerns about his weight and had not dieted. He usually wrestled two weight classes below his off-season weight, and his coach strongly recommended he diet. To make his weight, Mark had to diet stringently and induce vomiting. His history indicated that he had grown up in a dysfunctional family ruled by an alcoholic father. Family problems—most notably his father's drinking—were never discussed. Everyone in the family understood that they were to do whatever was necessary to avoid displeasing the father. Mark's bulimic behavior that had begun in wrestling became his way of managing his feelings about his father as well as most aspects of his emotional life. For this reason, he was unable to return to normal eating during the off-season like his wrestler friends. His alcohol use exacerbated the problem by increasing his depression and loosening his controls on eating. What began as a means to make weight for wrestling became a fairly serious eating disorder that lasted several years after he had stopped competing.

Identifying Athletes With Bulimia Nervosa

The primary difficulty in identifying athletes with bulimia is the same as that in identifying nonathlete bulimics; they tend to be at or near normal weight. Additionally, many tend to be social and are adept at hiding their emotions and their disorder. For these reasons, the sport management team must be able to recognize the signs of bulimia nervosa, which are often more subtle than those of anorexia. These signs include physical and psychological/behavioral characteristics. As with anorexia, the presence of some of these characteristics does not necessarily indicate the presence of the disorder. However, the likelihood of the disorder being present increases as the number of characteristics increases.

Physical Symptoms of Athletes With Bulimia Nervosa

1. Callus or abrasion on back of hand from inducing vomiting
2. Dehydration, especially in the absence of training or competition
3. Dental and gum problems
4. Edema, complaints of bloating, or both
5. Electrolyte abnormalities
6. Frequent and/or extreme weight fluctuations, especially with resultant mood fluctuations (i.e., mood worsens as weight goes up)
7. Gastrointestinal problems
8. Low weight despite eating large volumes
9. Menstrual irregularity
10. Muscle cramps, weakness, or both
11. Swollen parotid glands

Psychological and Behavioral Characteristics of Athletes With Bulimia Nervosa

1. Binge eating
2. Agitation when bingeing is interrupted
3. Depression
4. Dieting that is unnecessary for appearance, health, or sport performance
5. Evidence of vomiting unrelated to illness
6. Excessive exercise beyond that required for the athlete's sport
7. Excessive use of the restroom
8. Going to the restroom or "disappearing" after eating
9. History of sexual abuse

10. Self-critical, especially concerning body, weight, and sport performance
11. Secretive eating
12. Stealing, especially when items taken are related to bulimia (i.e., food, laxatives, etc.)
13. Substance abuse—whether legal, illegal, prescribed, or over-the-counter drugs, medications, or other substances
14. Use of laxatives, diuretics, or both that is unsanctioned by medical or training staffs

Effects of Bulimia Nervosa on Sport Performance

As with anorexia nervosa, bulimia nervosa negatively affects sport performance as a result of its physiological and psychological complications. Also, the nature and magnitude of these effects are influenced by the same factors involved in anorexia nervosa—severity and chronicity of the disorder, individual differences in the athlete, and the physical demands of the athlete's sport.

Physiological

Most physiological problems of bulimia nervosa that interfere with sport performance are usually a direct or indirect result of purging and may be exacerbated by malnutrition. The most important of these are probably dehydration and electrolyte abnormalities. Because the body is 60% to 70% water, a well-hydrated body performs more effectively than a dehydrated one. In fact, probably no single nutrient deficiency can negatively affect sport performance as quickly as insufficient water, because the first symptom of dehydration is fatigue (Whitney & Hamilton, 1984). Fluid loss through dehydration can also affect body temperature regulation in that fluid serves to cool the body in the form of sweat. Also, poorer sport performance accompanies dehydration because fluid loss can result in a reduction of blood volume, which in turn can reduce oxygen-carrying capacity, aerobic capacity, and endurance (U.S. Olympic Committee, 1987). Relatedly, the previously mentioned study by Webster et al. (1990) involving dehydration techniques that wrestlers often use found that these techniques reduced upper-body strength and decreased anaerobic power and capacity. We can probably generalize the results of this study to other sports and athletes.

Unfortunately, dehydration (purgation) causes the loss of not only water but necessary electrolytes as well. The loss of fluid and electrolytes through dehydration can account for most of the physical symptoms that inhibit sport performance. In addition to fatigue, these usually include muscle weakness, muscle cramps, loss of coordination, excessive thirst, and dizziness. Other symptoms that may have a less direct effect on performance (as a result of making the athlete feel "heavy") include rebound water retention or edema and constipation.

Finally, as mentioned previously, the bulimic athlete may be dieting stringently and purging most of what she eats. In this case, malnutrition becomes a factor just as for the anorexic athlete. Malnutrition may not only exacerbate the aforementioned symptoms, it may also place the bulimic athlete at risk for the same performance-inhibiting complications discussed earlier for the athlete with anorexia nervosa.

Psychological

Probably the prime contributors to poorer performance in the psychological/emotional realm relate to the bulimic athlete's emotional instability (mood swings and unevenness of mood), especially depression and low self-esteem. The anorexic athlete's problems with concentration discussed earlier also apply to the athlete with bulimia nervosa. Her concentration, which is already affected by her obsessions with her weight, body, and eating, is further decreased as a result of depression, thereby making mental mistakes more likely to occur. Depression can also create psychomotor retardation, which slows the athlete both mentally and physically. It can also decrease motivation and lead to lower activity and energy levels. Depression, low self-esteem, and a sense of ineffectiveness tend to lower the athlete's self-confidence and can make her thinking more negative. Unfortunately for the athlete with bulimia nervosa, many of the necessary psychological components of successful sport performance—concentration, motivation, confidence, and playing with emotion—are the ones most apt to be negatively affected by the disorder. Thus, she finds it more difficult to use the emotional part of herself in a helpful way.

Eating Disorder NOS and Other Eating Disturbances

It is well documented that many athletes engage in pathogenic weight loss practices (e.g., Black & Burckes-Miller, 1988; Dummer et al., 1987; Rosen & Hough, 1988; Rosen et al., 1986) that are actually symptoms of anorexia nervosa or bulimia nervosa. However, many of these athletes do not meet enough diagnostic criteria to warrant diagnosis of either disorder. Obviously, some of these individuals do in fact meet enough eating-disorder criteria to be diagnosed as having an eating disorder NOS, and these individuals are as much in need of treatment as those who are given the diagnosis of anorexia nervosa or bulimia nervosa. Even though eating disorder NOS is discussed significantly less than anorexia and bulimia in the eating disorder literature, this does not in any way mean that it is any less important. Eating disorders NOS can be quite serious and debilitating. Additionally, as suggested earlier, more individuals may actually meet criteria for the diagnosis of eating disorder NOS than for anorexia nervosa or bulimia nervosa.

Subclinical Variants

There are also many athletes who, despite reporting the use of induced vomiting, laxatives, diuretics, and fluid restriction in an effort to lose weight, do not technically meet the criteria for a diagnosis of an eating disorder. In other cases, an obvious eating disturbance does not involve these pathogenic methods. For example, one athlete typically ate less than 600 calories a day because she believed she was "fat," especially in her hips and thighs. She also tried to avoid weight training her lower body for fear that she would "just get bigger." In actuality, her weight was within a normal range for her height and body frame. She was unhappy much of the time but was seldom what one would term depressed. Her concerns were complicated by fairly significant family problems.

The athlete just described was certainly displaying an eating disturbance. Even though the disturbance was probably a subclinical variant of anorexia nervosa or bulimia nervosa, she would not be given the diagnosis of either disorder. Depending on the circumstances operating at the time of her evaluation, she may not even have met the criteria for eating disorder NOS. The severity and debilitating effects of these disturbed eating behaviors vary among athletes. Apparently, some athletes, like most wrestlers, can practice these behaviors with few long-term negative effects. For many other athletes engaging in these subclinical or subthreshold behaviors, however, it may simply be a matter of time before their eating disturbances, progress (regress) to the point that they become full-blown clinical disorders. If an individual does have the predisposing factors for an eating disorder, the likelihood that she will develop the disorder increases if she experiments with restrictive dieting and pathogenic weight loss behaviors.

In many ways, whether the individual meets all the diagnostic criteria for an eating disorder is irrelevant. As we mentioned in an earlier chapter, even though certain criteria are necessary for a diagnosis, an individual does not have to meet these criteria to warrant treatment. An athlete willing to put herself at risk by using potentially dangerous weight loss methods could probably benefit from treatment. In fact, early detection and intervention may preclude the development of the full clinical eating disorder in these individuals, thereby making successful treatment more likely.

Conclusion

Athletes with eating disorders are probably more similar than dissimilar to their nonathlete counterparts. As one might expect, most of the dissimilarity is related to the sport itself or to the sport environment that surrounds it. Though in some ways this dissimilarity seems to favor the athlete, in many others it probably places the athlete more at risk for developing an eating disorder, primarily because sport can legitimize the drive for suboptimal weights and implicitly endorse the use of pathogenic weight loss methods. For the athlete who is predisposed to an eating disorder, pursuing a low weight and using pathogenic means to lose weight serve not only to precipitate the eating disorder but also to maintain it once it has been initiated.

Apparently, some athletes can tolerate the effects of their disorder for extended periods and can even achieve considerable success in their sport. Typically this success is short-lived in that sport performance declines over time as a result of the serious physiological and psychological complications of anorexia and bulimia nervosa. Even if performance does not decline quickly, eating disorder–related injuries or illness may significantly curtail or prevent athletic competition. The negative effect that eating disorders seem to have on sport performance makes us wonder why athletes continue to use and coaches continue to encourage or allow the use of pathogenic weight-control methods in the quest for suboptimal weights.

This chapter painted a picture of the athlete with an eating disorder. The physical and psychological effects that we've seen clearly indicate the need for prompt treatment of affected athletes. In the next chapter, we will discuss how the sport management team can best manage the complex and sometimes difficult process of getting the athlete with an eating disorder into treatment.

CHAPTER 5

Managing Athletes With Eating Disorders: Treatment-Related Issues

Once the sport staff suspects an athlete has an eating problem, many management issues will arise. For our purposes, the term "management" refers to a general process that begins with identifying the problem and continues through the final stages of aftercare treatment. More specifically, it involves referral and arrangement for treatment, implementation of the therapeutic regimen, monitoring specific therapeutic strategies, and arranging for follow-up or aftercare treatment to ensure that the athlete maintains his or her therapeutic gains.

Although we will focus primarily on management in this chapter, such a discussion will be more meaningful and helpful within the context of treatment. We strongly recommend that the formal treatment of athletes with anorexia or bulimia nervosa be undertaken only by qualified mental health professionals who are experienced in treating eating disorders. Ideally, these individuals should also be familiar with, and have an appreciation for, the sport environment.

The term "treatment" refers to the application of therapeutic techniques in an attempt to modify the behavioral, cognitive, and affective components of the athlete's eating disorder. Treatment is distinguished from management in part by who is involved and what they do. Formal treatment involves only the health care professionals who are providing therapeutic services. Management, on the other hand, is certainly an integral part of treatment and can in some cases involve interested and concerned individuals in the sport environment such as coaches, athletic trainers, team physicians, sport psychologists, and exercise physiologists, who make up what we call the sport management team. The involvement of these people is to occur only under certain conditions. First, the athlete must consent to their involvement. Second, this involvement must be therapeutic as defined by the mental health professional coordinating the athlete's treatment. Finally, it can occur only within acceptable ethical guidelines regarding protection of the athlete's confidentiality and privacy.

Coaches and other members of the sport management team have tremendous power with their athletes, as dance instructors can with their dance students. We believe that these individuals will exert this power regardless of how formally involved they are in the management process. Unfortunately, their power can be negative. To help the athlete as much as possible, we obviously want to try to maximize the positive nature of this influence while minimizing its potential negative aspect. This is more likely to occur when the sport management team is part of an organized management effort orchestrated by the health care professionals who are handling the athlete's treatment. We will therefore emphasize in this chapter when and how these individuals can most effectively be involved in the management process given the conditions mentioned earlier.

Approach and Referral

Approaching an athlete who is suspected of having an eating disorder in an effort to make a referral for treatment is difficult. As we discussed previously, individuals with eating disorders try very hard to appear perfect and have an intense fear of displeasing others. Relatedly, they use denial as a primary defense. Anorexic athletes often believe that they have no problem and thus are likely to deny the existence of a disorder. Individuals with bulimia nervosa usually deny engaging in disturbed eating to avoid embarrassment and possible disapproval by others. In addition, athletes may fear that in treatment they will be forced to eat or will be prevented from purging. In either case, they assume that they will gain weight, which they believe will lead to an inevitable sequence of negative consequences they cannot tolerate, not the least of which is decreased sport performance. Finally, athletes may fear that if a disorder is confirmed, they will not be allowed to compete. This has serious implications for the individual's self-esteem, most of which stems from his or her identity as an athlete. It may also set the athlete apart from the rest of the team.

Approaching the athlete about treatment requires great care and sensitivity. Athletes compose a special population regardless of their eating habits. As such, they require special consideration when we communicate with them.

General Considerations in Working With Athletes

We hear many athletes complain about how sport support staff sometimes deal with them. One of the most frequent complaints is that they are often treated as "just an athlete" or a "body" rather than as a person. Being an athlete is certainly an important part of who the athlete is, but that is usually only part of her identity. She does a lot more than just play a sport. As one athlete put it, "Athletes are people, too!" All people have feelings. If we fail to attend to the emotional part of the athlete, we may not know when she has a problem or what she needs.

Another complaint we hear frequently from athletes is that sport support staff often do not take their pain seriously. Athletes may believe that sport personnel think they are malingering—that nothing is really wrong and they are just lazy or faking injury to avoid practice. This can greatly affect an athlete; she may believe that her sport support staff is in essence saying that she is lying or has a character flaw. Sometimes the athlete is told that "the problem is all in your head." This response usually angers an athlete; it may disappoint or hurt her as well. Usually, the athlete is not malingering, faking, or lying. However, even if she were, that in itself would be an important communication the staff should respond to appropriately.

Coaches, athletic trainers, and team physicians need to attend to the athlete's pain, regardless of where it might come from. Pain is pain; in our work, we seldom try to distinguish between psychological pain and physical pain. Often physical pain can affect the individual emotionally through depression, anxiety, or fear. Just as often, psychological pain can have physiological effects, such as headaches, gastrointestinal problems, or insomnia. Pain is important, whether psychological, physiological, or both. Pain that has an organic base is the body's way of telling the individual that something is wrong. Psychic pain and physiological pain that has no organic base (psychophysiological) are the psyche's ways of telling the individual that something is wrong. It is important to respond to all of the athlete's reports of pain, even if it doesn't appear to be "real." We believe it is better to risk responding when nothing is wrong than to not respond when the athlete may actually have a serious problem.

By learning how to attend sensitively to athletes' emotions and to respond appropriately to their pain, members of the sport support staff increase both their knowledge of the athlete and the probability that any difficulties are detected early. Most important, however, this sensitivity can be instrumental in bringing about a positive outcome when someone needs to approach an athlete about a serious problem such as an eating disorder.

Approaching the Athlete

The most important issues in approaching the athlete suspected of having an eating disorder involve *who* should approach the athlete, *when* the approach is appropriate and necessary, and *how* best to approach to increase the likelihood of a positive outcome.

Who.   Typically, the best person to approach the athlete suspected of having an eating disorder is the individual who has the best rapport and the closest relationship with the athlete. This may be the head coach, an assistant coach, a trainer, the team physician, or any other individual in a position of authority or responsibility who is part of the sport management team. If no one feels especially close to the athlete, then the individual who feels most comfortable talking about emotional problems and who has an easy and comfortable interpersonal style is the best choice.

In most cases, a teammate should not be the one to approach the athlete. There are several reasons for this. Most important, a teammate is not likely to have the power that sport support staff has with the athlete, thereby making it easier for the athlete to dismiss the teammate's confrontation. However, even if a teammate were able to persuade the athlete to seek treatment, the affected athlete may then become too dependent on the teammate, or the teammate may feel obligated to, or responsible for, the athlete. Finally, a competitive relationship may exist between the two athletes regarding thinness or a position on the team. In such a case, the affected athlete is apt to be suspicious of the teammate's involvement.

It is important to remember that the encounter with the athlete in all likelihood will be difficult. The athlete typically will deny the existence of a problem or at least its seriousness. The person approaching the athlete should be prepared to get a negative response. If the team has a sport psychologist, he or she can provide guidance about how best to approach the athlete—what to say, what not to say, and how hard to push. Obviously, if the team has a sport psychologist, he or she could approach the athlete. However, we have found that sport psychologists or other mental health specialists are probably no more successful at producing positive referrals in these instances than sport personnel the athlete knows and respects.

When. Someone should approach the athlete as soon as an individual close to the athlete identifies a potential problem based on the presence of a number of the identifying characteristics listed in chapter 4. As we discussed previously, early identification of an eating disorder frequently results in fewer and less severe complications and less resistance to treatment, as well as a faster, easier, and more positive outcome of treatment.

How. Regardless of who approaches the affected athlete or when the approach takes place, the best strategy is usually to express concern for the individual and ask how he or she feels, both physically and psychologically. Even though the athlete's eating-related symptoms are very important in identifying the affected athlete, we do not recommend beginning by confronting the individual about these symptoms. Our experience suggests that sport personnel often regard the "evidence" (bingeing, purging, fasting, exercise, etc.) of the athlete's disorder as more important and helpful than it actually is in terms of getting the athlete into treatment. We think this is less important, because the athlete may deny having a disorder no matter how much evidence to the contrary is presented. The amount of evidence or the number of people presenting it often makes little difference to the individual if his or her need to deny is strong enough. *How* the evidence or confrontation is handled tends to be more important in producing a positive outcome.

Athletes suspected of having an eating disorder need to know that people care about them and will not criticize or embarrass them. They are more likely to believe this if the focus is on the athlete's well-being. If the individual approaching an athlete begins by talking about behaviors like bingeing, fasting, or purging, the athlete is likely to feel threatened and become defensive. This feeling may create more of a need to deny that a problem exists and will likely make the athlete less open to receiving assistance. We recommend a process characterized by maximal sensitivity and minimal invasiveness—a process that the athlete is not likely to experience negatively, whether he or she has an eating disorder or not. The athlete is being approached, not accused. When we approach an athlete, we are asking rather than telling, assessing rather than judging.

Persuading an individual with an eating disorder to accept a referral for evaluation or treatment is difficult under the best of circumstances. It is imperative, then, that the person approaching the athlete make as few mistakes as possible. Although the person must know what to do and how to do it in working to get the athlete in treatment, it is also important to know what *not* to do. Some caring and well-meaning individuals practice strategies that usually are not particularly helpful. In fact, employing these strategies may actually make the athlete less likely to accept a referral for evaluation and treatment.

One of the most detrimental errors a person can make in working to get a bulimic individual into treatment is following or watching her in an effort to catch her in the act of bingeing and purging. This vigilance is usually well intended; some people believe that "catching" the bulimic can help her stop her symptoms, or that they can use the information they have collected to persuade her to seek treatment. Unfortunately, this vigilance only puts more pressure on individuals with bulimia nervosa. It can make them seek even greater secrecy, and they often respond with an increase in bulimic symptoms. To individuals with eating disorders, this type of "help" makes them feel like they are being pressured or pushed. It usually has one of two negative outcomes: The individual who is doing the pressuring risks pushing the athlete away and perhaps losing her; or the athlete may push back with even more resistance, thus making her symptoms worse.

A similar strategy called "intervention" can produce the same negative results. This strategy is sometimes used in confronting individuals who abuse substances. Intervention typically involves several concerned people who as a group strongly and directly confront the affected individual in an effort to persuade (coerce) him or her to seek treatment. Although this strategy can sometimes be helpful with substance abusers, it can have very negative effects on the individual with an eating disorder. This type of intervention can evoke such anger, fear, and embarrassment that the individual may become even more resistant to treatment, reject the people involved in the intervention, and feel more pressure to "go underground" or become "invisible."

Identification Issues

The difficulties associated with approaching an athlete may differ based on the disorder. The athlete with anorexia nervosa is often relatively easy to identify due to the significant weight loss that typically accompanies the disorder; the evidence that an eating disorder exists is almost irrefutable. Because the presence of bulimia nervosa in an athlete is often more difficult to identify, approaching this athlete has complications specific to the disorder. As we discussed earlier, the individual with bulimia nervosa can be at any weight. In that bulimia is usually a quite secretive, almost invisible disorder, identifying the bulimic individual is even more difficult. Relatedly, more difficult identification often makes for a more difficult referral. Individuals with anorexia nervosa cannot hide their extreme thinness (although they often try to by wearing very baggy or oversized clothing), and one can verify their low weight and extreme weight loss by simply challenging them to be weighed. Even though the individual with anorexia can maintain that she does not have a problem, she finds it more difficult to deny her low weight. The individual with bulimia nervosa, however (unless she has been discovered bingeing and purging), can simply claim that she is not engaging in bulimia-related behaviors. Thus, it is often easier for the athlete with bulimia nervosa to refuse a referral for treatment.

Another issue regarding identification is the possibility of incorrectly assuming that an athlete has an eating disorder. Although we very much want to protect the individuals involved from undue stress or difficulty, we don't think incorrect identification is particularly serious. Some people may assume that mistakes are frequently made in this regard and that these mistakes are troublesome or even harmful to the individual who is incorrectly identified. It has been our experience, however, that if an eating disorder is suspected, it is usually present, and that incorrectly identifying athletes as possibly having an eating disorder in most cases carries little risk or difficulty for the people involved if those approaching them have treated them in a respectful, sensitive manner while protecting their privacy and confidentiality. In fact, in the few such cases that we have been involved in, the the individuals showed little if any resistance to undergoing an evaluation. This lack of resistance can be helpful in making the diagnosis, usually indicating a low probability that a disorder is present.

Admission of a Problem

In some ways, admitting to having an eating disorder is much more threatening for the person with bulimia nervosa than for the person with anorexia nervosa. The individual with anorexia is dieting stringently and is significantly underweight. The individual with bulimia is bingeing—often eating large volumes of food—and then purging the food, usually through self-induced vomiting or self-induced diarrhea through the use of laxatives. Clearly, the anorexic's set of symptoms is more socially acceptable and more acceptable to the affected individual. In fact, many individuals with bulimia nervosa regard their disorder as a "disgusting habit." For this reason, and because bulimics need to be perfect and to please others, admitting to engaging in bulimic behaviors can be quite threatening. As a result, it is very difficult for these individuals to accept a referral for treatment.

If an athlete will admit to having a problem (whether specific to eating or more general), the person who has approached her can gently suggest that it might be best to have a consultation with a specialist. Then arrangements should be made for the athlete to see an eating-disorder specialist who can provide a thorough evaluation. The athlete is more likely to accept the idea of going for a consultation than committing to ongoing treatment. An appointment for the evaluation should be made as soon as possible because the athlete's fear and ambivalence about treatment may make her change her mind if given the opportunity. In fact, we recommend that the athlete call for the appointment when she admits the problem and while the referring person is present. It goes without saying that the athlete's freedom in accepting an appointment should in no way be restricted by sport commitments. For example, if the first available appointment occurs during normal practice time, the athlete should be excused from practice. It is imperative that the sport management team make it as easy as possible for the athlete to comply with treatment.

An athlete who agrees to the evaluation may inquire about exercise, training, and competition. These are not questions to be answered by sport personnel. Athletes should be told that the professional health care providers who will be doing the evaluation must make all decisions about sport participation.

Getting the athlete to accept a referral for an evaluation is sometimes a significant accomplishment in itself, but getting him or her to then participate in formal treatment may be quite another challenge. However, if the presence of an eating disorder is confirmed in the evaluation, then the eating-disorder specialist providing the evaluation can play a major role in convincing the athlete of the need for treatment and can begin to motivate the individual for treatment.

Refusal of Treatment

For a variety of reasons, some athletes deny the existence of a problem and resist or refuse a request for an evaluation, regardless of how they are approached. The major concern when an athlete refuses treatment involves the continued and increased risk to his or her physical and psychological well-being. To minimize this risk, it is imperative that these athletes be induced to accept treatment as soon as is reasonably possible. In this section, we recommend ways that the sport management team can best manage these athletes.

Initial Refusal

If the athlete does not accept the initial referral or does not even admit that a problem exists, it is probably best not to push too hard at this point unless you believe the athlete is at risk medically. Schedule a medical examination at this point to determine her risk in this regard. If the athlete refuses this examination, prohibit training and competition until she undergoes such an examination. If after this examination the athlete's physical health is found to be compromised due to the disorder, she is to be prohibited from practicing or competing until she agrees to be evaluated by an eating-disorder specialist. If the medical examination and laboratory testing determine that her health is not being compromised by the disorder, the examining medical personnel can again suggest that she seek an evaluation regarding her disorder. If she still refuses, it is probably best to wait before approaching her again.

After a short time—perhaps 2 to 3 weeks—the athlete should be approached again. It is even more important now that the person approaching her show sensitivity and concern. Avoid direct confrontation or coercion for as long as possible. Coercion tends to make the athlete more fearful and angry, possibly resulting in more resistance. If she still refuses, we again advise waiting. After another short period, repeat the process.

Continued Refusal

Even after all of the referral procedures we've recommended have been followed, the individual may still resist accepting a referral or admitting to an eating problem. Obviously, this situation calls for a more direct confrontation. The best strategy at this point involves attempting to create doubt on her part that she is not at risk. For example, if others have seen or heard her purge, tell her this. If her weight is low, ask her how much weight she has lost in recent months. Give her information concerning a healthier weight. Ask her if she has lost her menstrual cycle; is having difficulty sleeping; or is feeling depressed, weak, tired, or irritable. If she admits to these problems, suggest that they may all be related to her eating habits. It is imperative that this confrontation not convey anger or criticism. A confrontation that feels critical to her will only increase her fear and need to resist. Let her know that you are concerned about her eating and weight because they may reflect an emotional or physical problem.

If the athlete continues to maintain that she does not have a problem despite the evidence presented to the contrary, then you may need to verify the accuracy of the information you have about her eating difficulties. If the evidence is clear that she does need treatment, then the appropriate individual must firmly but gently insist that an evaluation be scheduled. Although this is sometimes necessary, we try not to use insistence until we have tried all other avenues without success.

Prohibit Athletic Participation

Even though the athlete's refusal to have an evaluation can present a complex and difficult problem for the sport management team, the solution is actually simple, though its effective implementation will likely be difficult. The athlete is not allowed to practice or compete until she agrees to the evaluation, but as a part of the team or program she must still attend practices and competitions. The difficulty in implementation comes when the athlete refuses the psychological or medical examination. How is this to be handled? Should she be suspended from the team or program until the evaluation takes place?

Suspension is an option, but it should usually be a last resort for several reasons. First, even if the athlete is suspended, she may train on her own, which in some cases may be more dangerous than continuing to work out with her team because no one will be monitoring her exercise. Second, denying the athlete the opportunity to participate in her sport may deprive her of the only source of positive feelings and self-esteem in her restricted and unhappy life. Third, control is a key issue for the individual with an eating disorder. She may view her suspension as an attempt by others to control her. If so, she may respond with frustration as well as increased resistance. It may sound as though we are implying that suspension should not be implemented in these cases, but that is not our point. If all attempts to persuade the athlete to agree to an evaluation fail, you have no alternative but suspension.

Fortunately, you can try several strategies before reaching the point of suspension. Many of these involve communication, and we have discussed some previously in the section on making a referral. One very important addition to those already mentioned is to help the athlete understand the motivation for the threatened suspension. Communicate your concern for her physical and emotional well-being. Stress to the athlete that suspension is not designed to be a punishment, even though it may feel like it. Rather, it is simply a way of showing concern. Emphasize that as much as everyone would like for her to be on the team and compete, that is not as important as her physical and emotional well-being.

In addition to explaining the reason for the suspension, you need to convey several important messages to the athlete. First, stress that you understand her resistance to the evaluation. Then tell her that it is easy to understand that she feels the threat of suspension is an unfair ultimatum. The athlete needs to know that her anger about this threat of suspension is understood and accepted. In addition, let her know that the suspension and all of her feelings that surround it are worth risking, but that her health and life are not. Even though the athlete will still not like this situation, she may like this expression of concern and respond positively to it. Finally, if an athlete with an eating disorder is to respond positively to concern expressed for her health and happiness, this concern must be communicated in such a way that the athlete perceives it as concern rather than control. Genuine caring and concern sometimes feel like control to the individual with an eating disorder—a control she may need to resist for a variety of reasons. Under no circumstance is this more critical or more likely to occur than when the athlete refuses evaluation or treatment and must be suspended.

Suspension

If all efforts to persuade the athlete to be evaluated fail, the appropriate individual (i.e., the coach) should invoke the suspension. Again, this calls for a firm but gentle approach, and the athlete should be told that she will be welcomed back to the team or program once she agrees to follow through with an evaluation. If she stays away from practices and competitions, someone from the sport support staff should contact her on a fairly frequent basis (every week or two), and again encourage her to have the evaluation.

Treatment Dropout

Another difficult situation involves the athlete who begins treatment but drops out before treatment has been successfully completed as determined by the health-care professionals working with her. Many individuals with eating disorders for a variety of reasons prematurely terminate treatment. If this happens, the appropriate sport-related personnel should encourage the athlete to return to treatment. If she refuses despite all efforts to persuade her to return, the coach should invoke suspension in the manner described earlier.

Family Involvement

The athlete's family may be involved in the process of getting the athlete into treatment. One factor affecting this involvement is the athlete's age—the younger the athlete, the more the family's involvement is recommended. Certainly, one would anticipate more involvement with younger athletes. We must also consider several other issues when involving family members. The first involves the athlete's right to privacy. Many individuals with eating disorders do not even want their families to know about their disorders much less have them involved in the treatment process. Should family members be involved if the athlete requests that they not be informed of the suspected difficulty? This is a very delicate and complex issue. As we will discuss later in this chapter, some ethical questions arise in this regard, at least for the health care practitioners who are providing treatment. The issue for sport personnel, however, involves ethics less than it does relationships and trust. By involving family members against the athlete's will, sport personnel risk angering and perhaps alienating the athlete. However, if these concerned personnel believe that the athlete is at significant risk and that family involvement could assist in the situation, they should take the risk of informing the family. However, before doing so, the sport personnel should fully explain to the athlete why family members must be notified and when this will take place.

Although family involvement can sometimes facilitate getting an athlete to agree to an evaluation or treatment, it can also make for potential problems. Remember that the family plays a role in the development of an eating disorder; certain familial characteristics help predispose the individual to the disorder. The family, particular family members, and family issues or problems may also play significant roles in the maintenance of the athlete's disorder. As a result, family members may not respond well to being informed of the athlete's disorder. Like their son or daughter, parents may deny that a problem exists. Or, depending on how involved parents are with their son's or daughter's sport performance, they may not support the decision to withhold sport participation or suspend the athlete. It is also possible that the relationship between the athlete and family members is so negative that family involvement may create more difficulty for the athlete. In some cases, the athlete may resist more if his or her family is working to facilitate treatment.

An exhaustive discussion of the issues related to family involvement is well beyond the scope of this book. Suffice it to say that despite all the negative possibilities associated with family involvement, we strongly recommend that family members be involved whenever feasible. Regardless of the relationship between the family and the athlete, the family is a very powerful force in the athlete's life. With the family formally involved, the mental health professional coordinating treatment can have more control over the potential effects of this involvement—minimizing the negative effects while maximizing the positive ones.

Treatment Issues

Treatment for the athlete who agrees to participate can involve a variety of types and modes and may vary as to goals, duration, and intensity. In this section, we will discuss different types of treatment and what the athlete can expect as he or she begins the treatment process.

Inpatient Versus Outpatient

Treatment for an eating disorder can involve either inpatient or outpatient treatment, or both. The decision regarding the appropriate treatment mode for the athlete is usually made by the professional health care providers involved in her care. Generally, most individuals with anorexia nervosa require at least some inpatient treatment, although the health care provider may try outpatient treatment if the individual's weight is stable and not extremely low and she is not purging (Hsu, 1990). Conversely, most individuals with bulimia nervosa can and should be treated on an outpatient basis (Mitchell, 1990).

The decision to treat on an inpatient basis is usually made when the health care professional determines that the individual's physical health has been compromised to the point that she is medically at risk. It may also be made if the individual is too depressed to benefit from or cooperate with outpatient treatment, or if she is considered to be at risk for suicide or self-mutilation. The health care professional may try inpatient treatment even when the patient is not at risk medically or psychologically if an adequate trial in outpatient treatment has been unsuccessful. Also, on some occasions, an individual may be hospitalized at her family's insistence or in the very unlikely event that she herself requests she be hospitalized.

Types of Treatment

Whether the individual is in inpatient or outpatient treatment, he or she is likely to be involved in several modes of treatment. Typically, these include individual, group, and family therapy. Nutritional counseling and pharmacotherapy may also be included as adjuncts to the treatment regimen.

Individual. In individual psychotherapy, the therapist works only with the person with the eating disorder. The issues they deal with may vary somewhat depending on the therapist's particular theoretical orientation. Typically, the therapist tries to determine the exact nature of the individual's eating difficulties and how they might be most effectively changed. The therapist then tries to implement a change process. With anorexia nervosa, this most importantly involves weight restoration. For the individual with bulimia nervosa, this usually involves decreasing binge-purge behaviors while restoring more normal eating patterns. Other issues in individual therapy will differ based on the individual patient. Certainly, one issue that athletes need to deal with in therapy is how their sport or sport participation may be contributing to the maintenance of the eating disorder.

Group. In group therapy, the athlete will most likely be part of a group made up of other individuals with eating disorders. Group treatment can benefit the athlete in many ways, some of which are not possible in individual treatment. It allows the athlete an opportunity to discover that she is not alone—that others have a similar problem. It gives the individual a support group that understands her. Perhaps most important, group therapy provides a safe environment for the athlete to practice the new skills and attitudes she has learned not only from the therapist but also from the other group members.

Family. As the name implies, family therapy includes the patient and part or all of her immediate family, and in some cases extended-family members. The family rather than the individual is the focus of treatment. As discussed previously, the family usually plays a role in the development and maintenance of the disorder, and the disorder usually serves one or more functions in the family (Sherman & Thompson, 1990). A primary goal in family therapy is to modify maladaptive family interactions, attitudes, and dynamics to decrease the need for, or the function of, the eating disorder in the family.

Family issues and how they relate to the athlete's eating disorder are sometimes related to the patient's status as an athlete. For example, an athlete may believe that the only way she can gain her father's acceptance is through exceptional sport performance. As a result, the athlete may be willing to resort to the "heroic" methods of anorexia or bulimia to achieve and maintain a suboptimal or even unhealthy body weight. The modification of such a dysfunctional relationship between family needs, the eating disorder, and sport should be a focus in family therapy.

Nutritional Counseling/Dietary Guidance. This aspect of treatment is usually provided by a registered dietitian. Even though it is not usually referred to as therapy, it can be an indispensable part of a multimodal treatment approach. Individuals with eating disorders often believe that they are knowledgeable about nutrition, when in fact many aren't. They often know the calorie or fat content of particular foods but are much less aware of a food's nutrient density. Also, because they have practiced abnormal eating behaviors and their attitudes about eating are often based on myths and misconceptions, individuals with eating disorders seldom know what constitutes a balanced meal or "normal" eating. The dietitian's primary roles involve providing nutritional information and assisting in meal planning. Accurate information and the safety and control that the meal plan affords the patient can decrease the patient's apprehension about and resistance to changing her eating.

Pharmacotherapy. Pharmacotherapy, or drug therapy, is sometimes useful in the treatment of eating disorders, especially bulimia nervosa. Using pharmacological agents to treat patients with eating disorders tends to be a matter of clinical judgment by the treating psychiatrist. Drugs may be prescribed at any stage of treatment, depending on the patient's history, current functioning, or (lack of) response to more traditional therapeutic methods. The psychiatrist may prescribe medications to work directly on eating-related behaviors or less directly on conditions resulting from an eating disorder such as depression or anxiety. In the latter case, medication may reduce the patient's resistance to treatment or allow the patient to respond better to psychotherapy.

The issues of which patients should receive medication and when, as well as which medications should be prescribed, are numerous and complex and as such are well beyond the scope of this book. Team physicians or other medical personnel who need such information to monitor the athlete's medications during or following treatment should see Garfinkel and Garner (1987) and Mitchell (1990).

Treatment Goals and Expectations

Regardless of the type of treatment or who provides it, the primary focuses of treatment are normalizing weight and eating behaviors, modifying unhelpful thought processes that maintain the disorder, and dealing with the emotional issues in the individual's life that create a need for the disorder. For athletes with eating disorders, weight is an extremely sensitive issue and in many cases is the part of treatment that presents the most difficulty for them. In treatment, athletes who already are convinced they weigh too much may be asked to increase their weight significantly.

The health care professional treating the athlete will likely recommend a reasonable goal weight as part of the individual's therapeutic regimen. Typically, this is at least 90% of the patient's ideal body weight. Note here that we are referring to "ideal" as the weight recommended by standard weight charts rather than as defined by the athlete. Athletes with eating disorders may find this part of treatment more difficult than their nonathlete counterparts do. They have the same general concerns as nonathletes about increasing their weight, but they also have concerns from a sport standpoint. What they think is an "ideal" competitive weight—one that they believe helps them be successful in their sport—may be significantly lower than their treatment goal weight. As a result, athletes may have concerns about their ability to perform in their sport following treatment.

Although restoring the athlete's weight and healthy eating are the primary goals in treatment, other significant treatment goals tend to be less directly related to eating. For example, asking an individual with an eating disorder, especially someone with anorexia nervosa, to increase his weight is asking him to give up one of the primary means he has for dealing with the world. He uses it to protect himself, to feel in control, and to feel competent. He has practiced his disordered behaviors and rehearsed his unhealthy attitudes so often and for so long that to him they feel "right." Going against this will feel "wrong," and he is apt to feel anxious and afraid. In treatment, the athlete will need to be taught more helpful and positive modes of thinking as well as new, more effective, and healthier means of coping with his feelings.

More specifically, the athlete with an eating disorder needs to change the behaviors and thoughts that maintain the disorder. The behaviors involved typically include any behavior that is part of the individual's eating symptom complex, such as dieting, fasting, bingeing, purging, exercising, and weighing. They may also include using diet pills or engaging in any compulsive behavior used to maintain the disorder. The thoughts that need to change generally involve negative statements the athlete frequently makes to herself that help maintain depression and low self-esteem, as well as the cognitive distortions about her weight, body size, and eating that help her avoid eating or engage in bingeing or pathogenic weight loss methods such as purging. Equally important is the athlete's need to resolve existing emotional difficulties that fuel and perpetuate the disorder. These could include a myriad of issues related to family problems, sexual abuse, feelings of inadequacy and inferiority, dependency, low self-esteem, control, separation and individuation, and maturity fears.

Obviously, a thorough account of what goes on in treatment is well beyond the scope of this book. Stated briefly, for treatment to be effective, it should be as multidimensional as both the eating disorder itself and the individual who manifests it.

Duration of Treatment

An eating disorder may have taken a long time to develop. Consequently, it may take the individual a considerable length of time to recover from it. It may take months, or even longer. How long treatment lasts may be related to the diagnosis. Generally, anorexia nervosa requires a longer treatment time than bulimia nervosa. Certainly, the severity and chronicity of the disorder, regardless of type, affect the length of treatment, as do complicating personality factors that we will discuss in the next section.

The Health Care Professional

One of the most important issues related to effective treatment of the athlete with an eating disorder involves the health care professionals who provide that treatment. Certainly, the individual who is providing treatment is important, regardless of the patient's difficulties. When an athlete is involved, however, this may be even more important. Treatment can probably be more effective if the health care professionals working with the athlete have experience with, and an appreciation for, athletes and the sport environment. Someone who does not have this experience or appreciation may overlook or underestimate the significance of sports in the athlete's life. Granted, sports and athletes have sometimes been given too much significance. And some individuals who have not been a part of the sport environment may not consider the world of sports "real." To athletes, however, the sport world is very real. They may have trained for years in preparation to perform their sport. For many, their sport is their whole life, and being an athlete is who they are. The athlete's sport and identity as an athlete are often too important to be trivialized. A health care professional who does not consider and discuss the significance of the athlete's sport on his or her life before telling the athlete to discontinue the sport is not only unhelpful, but in many cases can also be antitherapeutic.

The athlete with an eating disorder very much needs and desires to be understood. This often involves understanding the role that sport plays in the disorder as well as the role it plays in the athlete's life. If the health care professionals treating the athlete fail to communicate this understanding, the athlete may feel she is not being taken seriously. This failure may create more doubt and resistance in an athlete who is already ambivalent about seeking treatment.

Complicating Factors

Under the best of circumstances, managing an athlete with an eating disorder before, during, and after treatment can be quite difficult. Factors specific to the individual athlete can further complicate management.

Personality Characteristics

Each person has a unique way of organizing the world and responding to the environment. The totality of these traits or characteristics is sometimes referred to as the individual's personality. In many cases, these personality characteristics can be very positive and helpful. Many athletes, for example, are committed, determined, hard-working, focused, and achievement-oriented, and these characteristics can help them function successfully in the realm of sports as well as in other areas of their lives. Some individuals, however—including athletes—have personality characteristics that are unhelpful, even self-defeating and counterproductive. These qualities can interfere with the management and treatment of an eating disorder, making resolution of the disorder even more difficult than it might be otherwise. Some of these characteristics are quite resistant to change and may persist in individuals even after they complete treatment.

Personality Disorders

Personality characteristics that are longstanding, inflexible, and maladaptive and that significantly interfere with the individual's everyday functioning constitute a personality disorder. Personality disorders not only interfere with treatment but also make it quite difficult for those around such individuals to deal with or manage them. Athletes with eating disorders who have these personality disorders are no different. Managing these athletes may be complicated by characteristics that manifest themselves in impulsiveness, irresponsibility, passive resistance, irritability, social withdrawal, ritualistic behaviors, lying, stealing, self-abuse, or suicidal behavior. These problems are difficult even for experienced therapists to deal with. Obviously, they are difficult for sport-related personnel to manage as well.

An understanding of these behaviors can facilitate management. Typically, these are behaviors the individual has practiced for years. They often relate to deficits in personality development, and the individual may have used them to manage her emotional life and relationships. It is important to realize that an individual engaging in these maladaptive behaviors may be doing the best she can given her personality and current state of functioning. Even though these behaviors are unhelpful to her, she is apt to have great difficulty changing them. Those working with the athlete must not take the behaviors personally. They are simply part of the disorder, whether it's related to eating or personality. Most likely, the athlete is engaging in the behaviors not simply to make life more difficult for those around her, but because she doesn't know what else to do.

Obviously, these individuals need help dealing with their maladaptive behaviors. It is difficult for us to make specific suggestions about managing these behaviors, because the response must be to the individual, not to the behaviors, and each individual is unique. In general, we again recommend the firm but gentle approach. In fact, when dealing with such behaviors, this approach is critical.

Confrontation and Discipline

Except for suicidal or self-destructive behaviors, most of these characteristics or behaviors can be managed through a firm but gentle confrontation. Some individuals are apprehensive about confronting someone who either has an eating disorder or has recovered from one; they fear making the person's eating problems worse. But if the athlete's maladaptive behaviors are interfering with her training or sport performance or that of her teammates, confrontation is acceptable. If these behaviors are putting her at risk physically or psychologically, confrontation is recommended. Confrontation is designed to change an individual's behavior in a positive direction. As discussed earlier, the person confronting the athlete cannot do so in such a negative way that all the athlete hears is criticism. For positive change to occur, the communication should be direct but fair and sensitive, focusing on the need for behavior change and providing a reasonable rationale for that change.

Relatedly, these maladaptive behaviors and their confrontation may require the administration of discipline. It is perfectly acceptable to discipline the individual with an eating disorder in the same fair and timely manner that you would any other athlete. However, we are stressing discipline, not punishment. Many individuals with eating disorders have already punished themselves more than enough. More punishment is the last thing they need.

Managing Self-Destructive Behavior

Obviously, individuals who are so depressed or distressed that they engage in self-destructive behaviors probably will not and should not be training or competing. If sport support personnel become aware of self-destructive behaviors on the athlete's part, they should not attempt to deal with them. Instead, the athlete should be referred immediately to the appropriate mental health professional.

Assuring Confidentiality

Confidentiality is designed to ensure the privacy of an individual in psychological treatment. Specifically, confidentiality in this context means that information regarding a person's emotional difficulty and treatment is released only on the patient's written authorization, and the information is released only to individuals who are specifically authorized to receive it. In this section, we will discuss the issues related to assuring the confidentiality of athletes in treatment for eating disorders.

Ethics

Most mental health professionals work under a code of ethics that basically provides total confidentiality to their patients unless a patient grants permission to the contrary. There are a few extreme exceptions to this rule, such as in an imminent life-or-death situation, when a court subpoenas a record, or when child abuse is involved. Of course, these situations rarely occur, especially among athletes with eating disorders, suggesting that in few situations is confidentiality broken.

Unfortunately, codes of ethics regarding confidentiality are often less clearly stated for sport-related disciplines. For example, a team's trainer can probably feel free to talk about having done rehab work on an athlete's injured ankle. But what about discussing that an athlete on the team is in treatment for an eating disorder? No formal ethical guidelines may exist to say that the trainer should not discuss this subject with anyone not involved with the athlete's treatment or not authorized to receive information. Nonetheless, it is important that the sport staff maintain the athlete's need for privacy and confidentiality.

Effect on Treatment

Not only is confidentiality important from an ethical standpoint, it may also have an effect on treatment. For athletes to complete treatment successfully, they must be able to trust the individuals involved in managing and treating their difficulties. A violation of confidentiality can destroy that trust.

The issue of confidentiality is extremely important to anyone receiving treatment for a psychiatric disorder, but it may be even more important to an individual being treated for an eating disorder. Part of this individual's concern about privacy or confidentiality relates to her need to be perfect as well as her fear of displeasing significant others. One reason many individuals avoid or refuse treatment is because they fear that others will learn of their difficulty (imperfection) and be displeased.

If treatment is to be effective, an individual seeking treatment must feel that she can express herself openly and freely. She is unlikely to do so if she believes that others, whether coaches, teammates, friends, teachers, parents, or the media, will discover aspects of her feelings, thoughts, or behaviors that she is ashamed of or embarrassed about. For these reasons, confidentiality becomes an issue that everyone involved in the athlete's management and treatment must understand and cooperate with fully.

Potential Problems and Recommendations

Some athletes may not want anyone associated with their sport to be involved in or to receive any information about their treatment. These athletes may need to have a special relationship with their therapist in which only the therapist is privy to certain information. Certainly, their request for privacy should be honored. In this situation, problems with confidentiality sometimes occur when interested people want information about the athlete or her treatment.

Sport-Related Personnel.   A coach or trainer may simply want to know whether an athlete is going to her appointments or if she is making progress in treatment. Other individuals involved in the athlete's sport may want more detailed information about specific issues. Sometimes the coach is concerned or worried about an athlete being in treatment; he or she may worry that treatment will change the athlete in ways that the coach would not support. In this instance, the coach may try to obtain information to allay his or her own anxiety.

What coaches and others want is immaterial. Issues of confidentiality relate to what the athlete wants, and more specifically to what he or she wants others to know. Again, information is not to be released without the athlete's consent. Under no circumstances should the athlete be coerced to give that consent. Additionally, if the athlete does not want anyone associated with his or her sport to be involved in treatment or management, coaches or other support staff should in no way hold this against the athlete.

In our experience, we have found that most athletes are willing to allow a coach or other support staff at least minimal contact with the therapist. Some others very much want the coach involved and view this as evidence of the coach's caring and concern. However, every athlete is an individual with individual needs. Thus, the role that the sport personnel play in the athlete's management and treatment must be determined on an individual basis. To reduce any chance of misunderstanding, the athlete should clearly and specifically express in writing all agreements about the type and extent of information to be released and who is allowed to receive it. An important part of this agreement should be that the athlete can at any time revoke this authorization to release information.

Teammates. Teammates of an athlete with an eating disorder are often aware of the problem and may also know that the athlete is in treatment. What should they be told in this situation? This matter should be handled as the affected athlete desires. If she wishes no information to be given about her disorder, her treatment, or her absence from (or return to) competition, the team and other sport personnel must comply. Again, her need for privacy about her disorder and treatment is of the utmost importance. The sport staff should respond to questions from teammates by answering, "I don't have any information that I can share with you."

Even though you cannot tell the teammates about the athlete's disorder and treatment, the sport staff should still listen to any information teammates may provide regarding their concerns about her. This information can help the professionals treating the athlete know when she is having difficulty. Acknowledge this information, however, without any confirmation that it is true. Simply thank the individuals for their concern. Confidentiality involves only the release of information; any input of information is certainly acceptable and is sometimes quite helpful in the treatment process.

Parents. For a variety of reasons, some people may not want their parents to know about their disorders or to be involved in their treatment. Therapists cannot release information even to parents without the individual's consent, except under the special circumstances discussed earlier and in the case of minors.

Although the conditions under which the mental health professional can release information are relatively clear, they are much less clear for sport-related personnel. Even though they do not work under the ethical constraints of mental health professionals, the sport staff must not act against the athlete's wishes about releasing information to parents without seriously considering the potential consequences. Probably the most serious consequence would be the athlete becoming very angry and displaying this anger through even more resistance to treatment or by leaving the sport environment entirely.

If after considering the relevant issues, circumstances, and consequences the sport staff conclude that parents should be apprised of the athlete's condition, we recommend several strategies. First, make another attempt to obtain the athlete's permission. If the athlete continues to object, tell her that her parents will be informed, explain why, and tell her what information will be released. Let her know when her parents will be informed. It is best to have the athlete present when the parents are given the information so she knows exactly what information has been released.

Media. Finally, how should the media be handled when a well-known athlete is noticeably absent from competition or returns following completion of treatment? Obviously, the athlete must be consulted about what, if anything, she wants released to the media. If she is not sure how she would like the matter handled, a good strategy is to say nothing until someone approaches the coach or other support staff with a specific question. Then it is probably best to have a coach or other sport-related individual in a responsible position issue a relatively innocuous statement that provides as little information as possible. You can simply report that the athlete needs time away from her sport and that she will return when she is ready to resume training. Garner and Rosen (1991) suggest viewing the athlete with an eating disorder as "injured." As a result, you can report that the athlete is injured and needs time to recuperate.

Regardless of how you handle this situation, rumors may circulate. Generally, we recommend not responding to rumors. In a special case in which some response is deemed necessary, we recommend that the designated spokesperson simply say that he or she can provide no information to confirm or deny the rumor.

Conclusion

We began this chapter with a discussion of how to approach the athlete in an effort to get him or her into treatment. This is perhaps the most important issue we deal with in this book; it is the very critical first step in what we hope is the process that leads to the athlete's recovery. The importance of getting the athlete into treatment was underscored by our recommendation of suspending sport participation to induce or motivate the resistant athlete to accept treatment. This recommendation supports our basic premise that the athlete's health and happiness are more important than his or her sport performance and that treatment should never be secondary to endeavors in sport—a point we repeat throughout this book.

Within this framework, issues related to treatment and management of the athlete with an eating disorder were discussed. We examined specific issues such as modes of treatment and goals and expectations. Some complicating personality factors that can make the process more difficult for all concerned were described. Finally, we discussed the importance of the delicate and complex issue of confidentiality and its necessary and appropriate application in the proper management and treatment of the athlete with an eating disorder.

In this chapter, we dealt primarily with management issues as they relate to the athlete's treatment and how the sport management team might best respond to these issues. In the next chapter, we will focus on issues that relate specifically to sport—issues that again may require changes in the behaviors and beliefs of the sport staff.

CHAPTER 6

Managing Athletes With Eating Disorders: Sport Issues

In the management of the athlete with an eating disorder, some issues that relate to the individual and to treatment are not specifically concerned with sport. The previous chapter dealt primarily with those issues, especially as they affected getting the athlete into treatment. In this chapter, we will focus on a variety of issues that are specific to the sport environment—issues that the sport management team will face once an athlete with an eating disorder has either begun or completed treatment. Unfortunately, there is a paucity of research in many of these areas. Consequently, much of our discussion is based on clinical experience, ours as well as that of other health care professionals and sport support staff we have consulted.

The most difficult and immediate sport issue that coaches and sport support staff face concerns decisions about training and competition. Little agreement exists about how to handle these issues. Those with a primarily mental health orientation probably tend to manage the athlete with an eating disorder more conservatively; that is, they are less likely to allow athletes to compete while they have prominent eating disorder symptoms or even after treatment. Those with a primarily sport orientation are probably more open to letting athletes with eating disorders compete when their symptoms are less severe.

In this chapter, we will present a management perspective that we believe best protects the athlete while taking into account the significance of sport participation in the athlete's life. Next we will look at how the sport management team can best handle the sport-related issues of weight management and eating. We will also discuss management strategies for sport support staff with respect to use of medication. Finally, we will examine the special circumstances of overtraining, staleness, and injury, and their possible relationship to eating disorders.

Training and Competition

Once the athlete has been evaluated and the health care professional has determined that he or she needs treatment, several issues that relate to training and competition arise. The most important question is whether the athlete should be allowed to continue to train and compete while recovering from the disorder.

Athlete Refuses Treatment

As we discussed earlier, individuals with eating disorders often fear treatment for a variety of reasons, and the athlete with an eating disorder is not likely to be significantly different. Despite the best efforts of the sport management team and the treatment specialists, an athlete may refuse treatment. If this happens, we believe that the athlete should not be allowed to exercise, train, or compete. In chapter 5, we recommended suspension for athletes who refuse to be evaluated for an eating disorder. We based this recommendation on the premise that the athlete's health takes precedence over sport performance, and without an evaluation it is difficult or impossible to determine accurately the athlete's health risk. The same premise and recommendation apply when an athlete has been evaluated, has been diagnosed as having an eating disorder, but refuses treatment. Accordingly, the same guidelines presented in chapter 5 regarding management of the suspended athlete also apply in this case. Most importantly, the coach should explain the reasons for the suspension to the athlete as well as what the athlete must do to have the suspension lifted.

Athlete in Treatment

In most cases, we do not believe the athlete with an eating disorder should compete, even if she is in treatment, until the health care professionals working with her decide it is safe for her to do so. This decision can come at any point during or following the treatment process and can also be reversed at any time. There are several reasons that the athlete should not compete until cleared to do so. First, depending on the nature and severity of the disorder, competing while eating disordered may place the athlete at greater risk medically or psychologically. Second, sport may play a significant role in the disorder such that the athlete's participation in sport may help to maintain or perpetuate it. In addition, allowing an athlete to compete while affected by an eating disorder may give her the message that sport performance is more important than her health.

Training and competition may also affect the treatment of an athlete with an eating disorder. Depending on the particular athlete and the specific issues, the influence can be positive or negative. On the positive side, in certain circumstances training and competition may motivate an athlete in treatment, a situation that we will discuss later in this chapter. On the negative side, however, training and competition may interfere with treatment by distracting the athlete. Treatment, especially if intensive, often requires the patient to invest considerable time, energy, and concentration. Some athletes may use training and competition as a distraction, particularly if they are not ready to get over the disorder. For example, an athlete might use sport as an excuse for missing treatment or for coming late to appointments or leaving early. She may use practice or an upcoming competition to rationalize not following her meal plan. Or she may rationalize weight loss or excessive exercise by claiming that she needs to make weight or get into better condition. She might claim that due to practice, a game, or traveling she did not have time to do her therapy homework. These distractions take the athlete's time, energy, and concentration away from treatment. Therefore, they may detract from what the athlete is able to receive from treatment.

Even though the athlete in treatment is not training or competing, she is not suspended and is still considered a member of the team, and she should attend practices and team meetings. It is important for the athlete to feel she is still part of the team; this allows her to maintain her identity as an athlete, and it also allows for a sense of attachment, of relatedness and rootedness—a sense that she belongs. Also, as Garner and Rosen (1991) suggested, you can consider the athlete with an eating disorder as "injured." As such, this individual is simply an injured athlete who is not training or competing until she is well. Obviously, teammates and the media will probably ask why she isn't competing. Certainly, this is a delicate situation that you can best manage by employing the strategies we recommended in the "Confidentiality" section of chapter 5.

Competing During Treatment

As stated earlier, we generally recommend that the athlete with an eating disorder not compete until the health care professionals handling her treatment decide that resuming competition is acceptable. For most athletes, this may not occur until treatment has been completed, or even later. Nevertheless, in some cases it may be permissible for the athlete to continue competing before successfully completing treatment; however, several important issues must be considered, the most important of which include diagnosis and the severity of the disorder.

Diagnosis. We see no circumstances under which an athlete meeting diagnostic criteria for anorexia nervosa should train or compete before successfully completing treatment. The medical risk to the athlete is simply too great. Although this is generally true for athletes diagnosed as having bulimia nervosa or eating disorder NOS as well, in certain circumstances it may be acceptable for some athletes with milder, more manageable forms of these disorders to continue training or competing before they have completed treatment.

Evaluation. The athlete with an eating disorder who is being considered for continuing competition while in treatment must undergo extensive medical and psychological evaluations. These evaluations must indicate that the athlete is not at risk medically and that competition will not increase her risk either medically or psychologically. Also, the health care professionals working with her must determine that sport participation will not play a role in maintaining the disorder or make it more difficult for the athlete to successfully complete treatment. If any doubt exists as to whether these criteria have been met, the athlete should not be allowed to compete.

Health Maintenance Standards.   If the athlete meets the criteria just mentioned, then bottom-line standards regarding health maintenance must be imposed to protect the athlete. The treatment staff determines these and individually tailors them according to the athlete's particular condition. These standards may vary by individual athlete or by sport. At a minimum, however, we believe the individual should maintain a weight of no less than 90% of his or her ideal body weight (as before, the term "ideal" refers to health rather than sport performance). Typically, this weight standard should be determined by a dietitian, who should also monitor the athlete's weight. Relatedly, we recommend that the athlete eat a minimum of three balanced meals a day, consisting of enough calories to sustain the preestablished weight standard the dietitian has proposed. More specifically, the dietitian should determine and monitor the meal plan. Based on research with amenorrheic athletes (Shangold et al., 1990; Stephenson, 1991; Wilson, Abdenour, & Keye, 1991), we recommend that women who have been without a menstrual cycle for more than 6 months undergo a gynecological examination to consider hormone replacement therapy. In conjunction with this recommendation, the team physician or an outside orthopedic consultant should monitor and evaluate bone density levels in women who are amenorrheic or who have had irregular menstrual cycles to assure that these athletes maintain healthy density levels. Obviously, if an athlete does not comply with eating criteria or fails to maintain minimal weight levels and healthy bone density, she must not be allowed to compete.

Additional Management Criteria.   Once the health maintenance levels have been established, guidelines regarding management and treatment have to be agreed upon by the health care professionals treating the athlete, the sport-related personnel who will be managing and monitoring her training and treatment compliance, and, of course, the athlete. These guidelines are designed to minimize the athlete's medical and psychological risks as well as to help management and treatment personnel be aware of any possible negative effects of competition or whether the athlete is complying with these standards. The following list represents what we believe are the minimal criteria in this regard: (1) To continue training or competing, the athlete must agree to comply with all treatment strategies as best she can; (2) the athlete must genuinely want to compete; (3) the athlete must be closely monitored on an ongoing basis by the medical and psychological health care professionals handling her treatment and by the sport-related personnel who are working with her in her sport; (4) treatment must always take precedence over sport; and (5) if any question arises at any time regarding whether the athlete is meeting or is able to meet the preceding criteria, competition is not to be considered a viable option while the athlete is in treatment.

Limited Training While in Treatment

If the criteria just mentioned for competing cannot be met, or if competition rather than physical exertion is a problem, some athletes who are not competing may still be allowed to engage in limited training. The same criteria used to assess the safety of competition (i.e., diagnosis, problem severity, and health maintenance) apply. Depending on the athlete and his or her particular circumstances, the health care professionals handling treatment could propose a limited training schedule in consultation with sport management staff. For example, some athletes for whom aerobic exercise is contraindicated may be able to do modified weight training. Practicing skills such as shooting for a basketball player or serving for a tennis or volleyball player might be acceptable. As with competition, if the athlete does not comply with all preestablished agreements about this limited training, or if this training in any way interferes with treatment or puts the athlete at risk, it must be discontinued.

Why Consider Competition or Training?

Even though we have taken measures to protect the athlete, why would we want to allow the individual to compete or train while she is experiencing eating-disorder symptoms? Our recommendation in this regard has little to do with sports or sport performance. Rather, it has to do with the athlete as a person and with treatment performance. We believe that continuing in their sport while in treatment has some advantages for some athletes.

In the previous section, we discussed how some athletes may use training and competing as distractions from treatment. Some athletes, however, may actually be motivated in treatment by the opportunity to continue training and competing. If the athlete is ready to get over her disorder, allowing her to continue with her sport with minimal risk when she really wants to continue can enhance her performance in treatment. The more positive the athlete is about treatment, the more benefit she is likely to receive from it. For some athletes, allowing them to train or compete gives them a small source of good feeling or self-esteem, perhaps the only one in their lives at this point. It may also let an athlete keep one of the few parts of her identity that is positive. This may help motivate her in treatment. Additionally, taking training and competing away from the athlete while she is in treatment may anger and frustrate her, making her more resistant to treatment. By informing the athlete of the health levels she needs to maintain to continue training or competing, you are giving her an opportunity to be in control. The decision about whether to train and compete rests with the athlete; she can be in control and compete as long as she takes responsibility for her health and meets those levels. Because eating disorders usually involve issues of control, taking this control can be an important first step in the athlete's treatment.

Finally, we believe that it is important to treat the individual with an eating disorder in her normal, everyday environment as much as possible. We accomplish little if her treatment is administered in an artificial environment (i.e., hospital) that gives her no opportunity to apply what she's learned in therapy to normal situations. We do not want her able to manage her difficulties only in the hospital or treatment office. If she is allowed to continue with her sport while in treatment, she can more easily apply what she learns to her sport environment.

Managing Teammates

Throughout this book, we have emphasized the need for sensitivity in dealing with the athlete with an eating disorder. At the same time, we must not forget about the affected athlete's teammates. Having a teammate with an eating disorder can create turmoil and difficulty for other members of the team. Some may worry about the individual. Others may be bothered, angered, or frightened by her eating-related symptoms. The athlete's symptoms may even cause other team members to question their own weight and eating practices. Team members who are upset by the affected athlete's behavior should talk with the coach and with the team's sport psychologist (if it has one) or with the mental health professional who is handling the athlete's treatment regarding possible solutions to this difficult situation.

Certainly, dealing with the athlete with an eating disorder requires sensitivity and understanding. The sport management personnel should extend the same sensitivity and understanding to other team members. If allowing an athlete with an eating disorder to compete while she's still displaying symptoms creates so much discord that it affects the emotional state or sport performance of others on the team, it is probably best to withdraw the athlete with the eating disorder from further competition.

Competition After Treatment

The first consideration of whether the athlete should be involved in training or competition after treatment involves her physical and psychological health. It is not unusual for someone who has completed a formal eating-disorder treatment program to still have symptoms of the disorder and to be in aftercare treatment. Even so, some athletes may be able to return to training and competition. Certainly, any athlete who still has medical or serious psychological complications of her disorder following treatment should not be allowed to exercise, train, or compete. In less clear-cut cases, the medical and psychological health care practitioners who have been treating the athlete must decide whether she should be allowed to resume training and competition.

Decision to Compete

Once the athlete has been medically and psychologically cleared to resume training and competition, several extremely important issues must be discussed and decisions made if the athlete's return to competition following treatment is to be successful. One of the most important issues involves whether the athlete really wants to return to competition. Some athletes may feel great pressure to return. Remember that they often have a need to please and a fear of displeasing significant others such as parents and coaches. Although they and their therapists probably dealt with these unhealthy or unhelpful needs and fears in treatment, they are unlikely to have fully resolved them.

Additionally, identity issues may also lead an athlete to competition when this is not what she really wants. She may remember her identity as an athlete and recall the small amount of self-esteem she occasionally enjoyed as a result of her sport performance. She may feel that she has no identity without her athlete status. Forming an identity will likely require a significant length of time and is apt not to have been completed by the time her formal treatment ends.

Why is the desire (or lack thereof) to compete so critical? If the recovering athlete chooses to compete only because she is afraid of not competing, she is doing something she doesn't want to do. This may make a successful adjustment more difficult. More important, however, she will be participating in a process that fostered and maintained the eating disorder. The more the athlete uses modes of thinking and behaving that are characteristic of the disorder, the greater the difficulty she will encounter in eliminating eating symptoms.

How do we ensure that the athlete's decision to compete represents what he or she really wants? The most obvious way is to ask. Ideally, the athlete will have learned to communicate more openly, directly, and genuinely while in treatment. As a result, she may be able to respond that she does not want to compete. When the athlete is asked this question, the significant others in her life (i.e., parents, coaches, or anyone she might be afraid to disappoint) must reassure her that it is all right for her to choose not to compete. They must let her know that they approve of her regardless of whether she competes. The athlete needs to know that she is valued for *who* she is rather than for *what* she does; she is important because of the person she is rather than for the physical prowess she displays. An athlete who decides not to compete may still need reassurance from sport-related personnel long after making this decision. Thus, it is important that these individuals be available to the athlete after the decision has been made.

Another way to ensure that the recovering athlete wants to compete is to let her make a tentative decision, one that she can change at any time. The athlete is not choosing to compete for a career or a season, but rather, to compete for one day, and then for another if all goes well. The athlete must be granted the opportunity to back away from competing at any point if she so chooses or if a problem arises. Knowing that she can opt not to compete at any time might make her decision easier. Typically, less pressure is associated with a decision made only for *now*—a decision that the athlete can revoke at any time.

What about the athlete who decides to compete and is unable to see that this is the wrong decision? By wrong, we mean that competing results in difficulties that the athlete is unable or unwilling to accept. These could include both emotional and medical problems associated with competition. In this case, it is probably best to have the mental health professional who has been involved in the athlete's treatment and the coach talk with her about the difficulties they see and inform her that competition is not a viable option. Obviously, this is a very difficult and delicate situation, and all our previous suggestions regarding the communication of caring, concern, and reassurance certainly apply here.

Finally, although the athlete's difficulties and feelings about the decision to compete are of primary concern, we must acknowledge as well the difficulties and feelings of the coach in this situation. Throughout this book we have emphasized how important a coach can be to an athlete. The athlete may be just as important to her coach. Often, a coach has invested significant time, energy, and money in a particular athlete. Given this investment, the coach may need to show considerable patience, understanding, and selflessness to respond as we have recommended.

Exercise and Training Issues

Athletes returning to competition after treatment will need to increase their exercise and training as they work themselves back into competitive condition. Of course, for this to happen, these athletes will need to be monitored very closely in terms of weight, eating, physical health, and psychological well-being. Although monitoring these areas is mostly the responsibility of the health care professionals working with an athlete, sport-related personnel can also play an important role. They are in an excellent position to collect information that might be less accessible to the health care professionals. For example, they can observe any excessive exercise or the athlete's physiological and psychological responses to training and competition. Consequently, their roles as monitors become increasingly important.

As the athlete increases her exercise and training during her attempt to return to competitive condition, coaches, athletic trainers, and the team physician must work in concert with the mental health professionals monitoring her aftercare treatment. This is especially true for the recovered anorexic athlete, for several reasons. First, more exercise means more energy expended. To maintain a healthy weight, the athlete needs to increase her caloric intake to maintain an energy balance in favor of her target weight that was established in treatment. Second, the athlete's exercise and training must be closely monitored. The return to exercise may evoke modes of thinking, feeling, and behaving that are reminiscent of the eating disorder. This may be explained in part by Epling and Pierce's (1988) contention that anorexia nervosa can be exercise induced, as we discussed in chapter 2. Also, the athlete had previously paired restrictive dieting and exercise as a way to maintain a suboptimal weight. If she begins exercising more intensely, it may feel strange for her to be eating. As a result, she may consciously or unconsciously reduce her caloric intake. Obviously, if exercise negatively affects the athlete's eating, it must be discontinued until the mental health professionals working with her feel it is appropriate for her to resume. The only way to determine whether exercise is affecting the athlete's eating may be to monitor her weight.

Competition Decisions

The issue of competition is an important one for the recovered athlete. Even if she has increased training and exercise to the point that she is in competitive condition physically, she may not be emotionally or mentally ready to compete. Having been away from competition, the athlete may have doubts about her ability. For any returning athletes with eating disorders but especially for those recovering from anorexia nervosa, part of this doubt may relate to competing at a weight higher than their competitive weight before treatment. It may also relate to low self-esteem. Typically, individuals with eating disorders tend to doubt they are "good enough" in most areas of life. Just as with most other salient treatment issues, the athlete and her therapist will most likely address and deal with self-esteem problems in treatment, but resolving them is apt to take some time following the end of formal treatment. Garner and Rosen's (1991) suggestion that these athletes be thought of as "injured" is an excellent one to keep in mind. The athlete and sport support staff need to think of the athlete as having been injured, realizing that it takes time for any injured athlete to recover and regain a competitive level.

Goal Setting.   Goals for competition are probably helpful for the athlete, and mental health professionals might provide assistance in setting reasonable goals. Most individuals with eating disorders have difficulty in this area; typically, they either set unrealistic achievement goals for themselves or come from environments in which unrealistic expectations have been set for them. Unrealistic goals can involve both the magnitude of achievement expected and the time necessary to reach such a level. Obviously, unrealistic goals lead to frustration and dissatisfaction. Setting realistic performance goals should be a cooperative effort involving mental health professionals, coaches, and, most importantly, the athlete. Again, coaches and the athlete need to view the athlete as "injured" and set goals for performance and competition accordingly, realizing that goals for optimal performance are unrealistic until the athlete has completely recovered. Following initial training trials and early competitions, the health care professionals, the sport management team, and the athlete should meet not only to assess the athlete's performance in relation to these goals but more importantly to provide support, reassurance, and encouragement until she no longer needs such meetings.

Issues With Specific Problems and Sports

Other issues affecting eating-disordered athletes' return to competition are specific to problem type—anorexia or bulimia. Earlier we stated the primary issue for the anorexic athlete—competing in a thinness-demand sport at a higher weight than she competed at before treatment. As she looks at her thinner competitors, she may feel out of place and that she has to compete at an unfair disadvantage (her higher weight).

Difficulties that relate specifically to the bulimic athlete often involve specific sports. For example, a recovered bulimic wrestler who returns to competition also often returns to an atmosphere and a mentality that will again put him at risk. His teammates will most likely be using the same dieting and dehydrating strategies that he was unable to manage. We believe that the recovered bulimic wrestler should not wrestle at a weight class that requires him to engage in "heroic methods"—eating and weight loss practices characteristic of anorexia nervosa or bulimia nervosa—to make weight. If the "normal" training and exercise necessary for wrestling do not lower his weight enough to enable him to wrestle in his designated weight class while he is eating enough to maintain at least 90% of his off-season weight, then that class is probably too low. To ask or to allow him to lose enough weight to compete at that class is risky. Even though he may have successfully completed treatment, he will most likely still be at risk for a recurrence of the disorder. Successful treatment means that he has become free of eating-disorder symptoms, that he now thinks differently about eating, weight, and, most important, about himself and his life. It also means he has learned new, more effective ways to manage his emotions. It does not mean, however, that he has developed an immunity to the disorder. If he reenters an environment similar to the one that helped foster and maintain his disorder and is then encouraged or allowed to engage in behaviors reminiscent of bulimia nervosa, he can very quickly and easily develop bulimic symptoms again.

Sports like swimming that require significant energy expenditure may also create problems for the recovered bulimic athlete who is attempting to return to competition. As she increases her training and thus her energy expenditure, she may need to eat more—perhaps significantly more than she has been eating in following her meal plan during treatment. It may be more reasonable and helpful to her not to increase her caloric intake significantly. Unfortunately from a training standpoint, this may mean that she is not able to increase her training very much. Will this affect her performance? It may, but you must remember that a possible increase in performance is not worth putting the athlete at risk. Even if she is able to increase her caloric intake significantly without difficulty during the season, she may then find it hard to reduce her intake during the off-season when the extreme energy expenditure is no longer necessary. For several reasons, it is better that her caloric intake not vary too much, regardless of the sport situation.

Treatment Priority

Earlier in this chapter we discussed the criteria necessary for the athlete who continues to compete while in treatment. One of these criteria was that treatment must always be given top priority. This priority is just as important for the athlete who is returning to competition following treatment. It is vitally important that sport-related personnel be aware of, and cooperate with, aftercare treatment goals. The athlete's physical and emotional well-being must continue to be of utmost importance; treatment is never to become subordinate to the sport as long as the mental health professional in charge of the athlete's treatment deems that treatment is necessary. For example, if the athlete needs or requests to be excused from practice or competition to attend treatment, the sport support staff must grant this request without resistance or reprisal. To do otherwise is to communicate to the athlete that sport is more important than her health. Even more important, perhaps, is that the athlete is never to skip meals to practice or compete. The athlete must have adequate time and opportunities to comply with the eating recommendations her meal plan dictates. Encouraging or allowing her to miss meals while using sport participation as a rationale is too reminiscent of the rationalizations she previously used to avoid eating.

Eating and Weight Issues

Related to the more general concern for the athlete's physical and emotional well-being is the specific goal of maintaining the athlete's weight in a therapeutic and healthy range. The health care professionals working with the athlete will have determined a reasonable weight during treatment (i.e., at least 90% of ideal body weight), and the individuals working with her must make every effort not to interfere with the maintenance of that weight. In this regard, the athlete will most likely continue to use a meal plan to guide her eating.

Meal Plan

It is important for most individuals with eating disorders—regardless of where they are in the recovery process—to follow a meal plan, for several reasons. From a treatment standpoint, the meal plan has been carefully arranged to meet the person's nutritional, medical, and psychological needs. Deviating from the plan may increase the likelihood of symptoms worsening in an athlete in treatment or returning in a recovering athlete. From the individual's standpoint, the meal plan may represent a sense of control with eating, and changes in that eating regimen may make the athlete feel less in control. For these reasons, it is best that the sport support staff not change the athlete's meal plan without consulting the mental health professional or dietitian who is working with the athlete.

Eating-Related Issues

Even if the athlete has completed successful treatment, she still may not be comfortable with certain eating circumstances. Remember, one of her greatest fears before treatment was probably related to eating. It may have taken years for this fear to develop. As a consequence, it may take a long time for her to adequately deal with and resolve this fear.

Team-Related Eating. The athlete's concerns about meals may involve simply eating with other people. Obviously, she will most likely be eating with teammates at pregame meals or while traveling. In these instances, the athlete is generally concerned that teammates and the sport support staff will watch her eat or that she will be presented with food that she is uncomfortable with or does not like but will be expected to eat.

With her apprehension that everyone is watching her, the athlete is apt to feel very visible and conspicuous. And to some degree, this is true—others will be watching. Most individuals with anorexia nervosa and some with bulimia nervosa are noticeably thin. As a result, they are equally noticeable when they have restored their weight. Coaches and trainers can make it easier for the athlete to get through this apprehensive phase by not commenting publicly about the athlete's weight and eating. The athlete very much needs to blend in to again become part of the team. Discomfort about others watching is usually quite normal; most of us would be uncomfortable if others were watching us eat. Feeling comfortable while eating with others is simply something she will have to achieve over time. Other people will stop watching as her eating normalizes; abnormal eating may be interesting to watch, but normal eating is quite boring. Probably the best way you can facilitate this process is not to comment during the eating circumstances. If there is cause for concern, have a talk with the athlete later in private. However, even this concerned gesture lets her know that she is being watched.

If the athlete is served food that for whatever reason she doesn't want to eat, the sport staff should try not to make too much of it. If the athlete doesn't eat it, allow this to be okay. Talk privately with her later to determine the nature of the difficulty and possible solutions to the problem. If she suggests that she'll eat something other than what her teammates are eating, a decision has to be made regarding how involved sport personnel want to be with this issue and how important it is. It must be decided whether she will be allowed to eat differently from her teammates. Other athletes may then demand to do the same. It may set her apart from her teammates and draw more attention to her eating. Our general recommendation is to have her do what her teammates are doing. However, if she does not want to eat, that should be acceptable. Obviously, if she has too much difficulty too much of the time, then she most likely is not ready to be competing and is in need of treatment. In this situation, the athlete needs a gentle recommendation that she contact her therapist.

Sometimes issues of concern to the athlete only indirectly involve her eating in the presence of others. For example, the athlete may worry that others assume she is vomiting when she goes to the bathroom after eating. As we discussed previously, the individual with an eating disorder very much needs to be accepted and as a consequence will sometimes worry about how others will respond to her, even after she completes treatment. Unless the evidence that she is vomiting is irrefutable, the best strategy for the sport support staff is to try not to attend to her behaviors after eating. Do not respond to her any differently than you would to anyone else who goes to the bathroom after eating.

Carbohydrate Loading. As mentioned earlier, carbohydrate loading is sometimes used in sports that require considerable endurance. If you recommend this strategy to the athlete's teammates, then it is acceptable to recommend it to her as well. It is important to treat her much as any other athlete is treated; this will help her feel more "normal" and accepted. At the same time, remember that she has probably tried to avoid foods high in carbohydrates. Thus, she may have difficulty integrating carbohydrate loading into her eating plan. It is best not to push if the athlete resists but simply to let her know that she can talk with members of the coaching or training staff about it if she wishes.

Eating "Diet" Foods. A potential problem in response to the athlete's eating occurs not with the athlete, but rather with those around her, such as coaches, athletic trainers, and teammates. It may then become a problem for the athlete. The problem involves the foods the athlete chooses to eat. During and following treatment, many recovering anorexics and bulimics continue to eat many of the foods they ate before treatment, not necessarily because they are low in calories, but because they like their taste. Others often label these foods as "anorexic" or "diet" foods; they are usually low in calories as well as in cholesterol, saturated fat, sodium, and preservatives. As such, they may be excellent food choices when part of a well-balanced meal plan. Nonetheless, when others see an individual who is recovering from anorexia or bulimia eat these foods, they sometimes assume that she is doing something wrong. As a result, they may become anxious, angry, or disappointed and then try to convince her to eat something else. This pressure to eat differently can be quite irritating to the individual. As long as she is maintaining her target weight through a balanced regimen that incorporates these low-calorie foods, and she shows no psychological, physiological, or behavioral correlates of anorexia nervosa or bulimia nervosa, there is no reason to respond to her choice of foods.

Monitoring Weight

In many instances, the sport management team's focus on weight only exacerbates the athlete's overconcern with weight. Unless the athlete's physical health or very low weight warrants monitoring, it is best to downplay weight and discourage weighing. If weighing is warranted, we recommend that it be done only by the dietitian or mental health professionals involved in the athlete's aftercare. This is important for several reasons. First, weighing is probably still a very sensitive issue for the recovered athlete. Thus, it should be handled by a health care professional experienced in managing such matters. Second, the athlete may have used the sport environment and the emphasis on thinness in that environment to rationalize or legitimize a suboptimal weight. Weighing in the sport environment by sport personnel may be too similar to earlier experiences that helped foster and maintain the eating disorder.

Our recommendation regarding weight involves using a target weight range rather than a particular weight. The lowest weight in the range is the lowest the individual can weigh and still be permitted to train and compete. The highest weight in the range is the weight that we do not want the athlete to exceed given her particular stage of recovery. If, for example, the range is determined to be 105 to 112 pounds, the individual is weighed using a physician's scale. The scale is set at 105 pounds; if the individual does not weigh less than 105, her weight is acceptable at the low end of the range. The scale is then set at 112 pounds; if she does not weigh more than 112, her weight is acceptable at the high end. Using a weight range rather than a specific weight helps reduce the individual's obsessiveness about a particular number and minor weight fluctuations that may occur as she recovers. If the athlete's weight falls into an unacceptable range, the athlete must stop training and competition until she attains and maintains the acceptable range.

Asking Individuals to Gain Weight

Although most of the athletes with eating disorders we work with have been asked to lose weight to enhance their performance, we sometimes encounter those who are being asked by their coach to gain weight to increase performance after developing an eating disorder. This typically occurs in non-thinness-demand sports such as basketball or softball. Usually the issue of weight centers on strength. A coach believes that the athlete would be stronger if she gained weight and therefore would perform better.

Just as with other athletes with eating disorders, we are assuming that the athlete being asked to gain weight to increase strength is not competing unless she has successfully completed treatment or that she meets all the criteria to continue competing while still in treatment. As mentioned previously, an athlete who has completed treatment or is still in treatment most likely has a meal plan and a recommended weight range. It is best to try to work with her within the parameters of the meal plan and recommended weight. Our recommendation in this regard is to consult with the athlete's therapist and dietitian in an effort to very gradually increase the athlete's weight to give her an opportunity to adjust to the increase.

If the increase in strength needs to occur quickly, methods that increase strength but do not involve weight gain should be attempted first. The athlete with an eating disorder tends to have more difficulty with weight gain than with other strength-enhancing regimens such as weight training. Also, just as a decrease in weight or body fat does not always increase speed or quickness or enhance other aspects of sport performance, an increase in weight does not always produce increased strength; other options may produce better results. It benefits this athlete to focus on something other than weight.

If the decision of all sport and health care professionals, and the athlete, is to have her increase her weight, expectations for weight gain should be tempered. Again, even if she has successfully completed treatment, she will probably have more difficulty gaining weight than an athlete who has not been eating disordered. Also, the sport staff should take strength measures throughout the process to determine if the athlete's strength is actually increasing as she gains weight. Once the weight gain no longer seems to be enhancing strength, the athlete should no longer be asked to gain weight based on the strength-enhancement rationale.

The criteria a coach considers in deciding competition status or playing time should be the same for the athlete with an eating disorder as it is for her teammates. If the athlete's competition status or playing time is reduced because she is not strong enough, the coach must tell her this and let her know what is expected if she wants her playing time to increase. If the coach does not let other team members play because they are not strong enough, the same standard should apply to the athlete with an eating disorder.

Medication Issues

Often, the medical or psychological complications of an eating disorder are not totally reversed or remedied by the time the athlete has completed formal treatment. If the returning athlete requires medication for complications of her disorder, this medication is probably best handled by the health care physician who prescribed it. In most cases, medication issues do not typically fall under the authority of sport-related personnel because the athlete with complications, especially medical ones, that are serious enough to warrant treatment with medications should not be training or competing.

Psychotropic Medications

As mentioned in an earlier chapter, individuals with an eating disorder are sometimes involved in pharmacotherapy as an adjunct to their treatment. The psychotropic medications they receive help them manage specific psychological symptoms such as depression or anxiety. Such drugs include antidepressants, antianxiety medications, and antipsychotic drugs. Some patients continue taking these medications following formal treatment. The health care physician who prescribed this medication should probably monitor it unless the team physician or other physician working with the athlete is experienced and comfortable with its use.

Probably the most commonly prescribed drug in the treatment of eating disorders, especially bulimia nervosa, is an antidepressant. An important issue with athletes concerns the side effects that some individuals experience while taking such a medication. Some antidepressants may produce dry mouth, constipation, or weight gain—symptoms that can interfere with the athlete's training and performance. If this happens, encourage the athlete to continue taking the medication as prescribed but to report these symptoms to the physician who has prescribed the medication or is monitoring it. The physician may be able to prescribe a different medication with fewer side effects that affect sport performance.

Cautions

Like other athletes, an athlete recovering from an eating disorder will occasionally request or require medication for a variety of physical symptoms, including gastrointestinal complaints. Specifically, the athlete may complain of constipation, diarrhea, bloating, stomachaches, or cramps. These symptoms may or may not be related to the eating disorder, and these instances can therefore create management dilemmas for sport physicians or trainers. Before administering medications for any of these complaints, they must consider the athlete's treatment history as well as the nature and origin of the complaint. Management strategies are more clear-cut in some situations than in others. For example, a recovering athlete who complains of constipation or bloating should not be given laxatives or diuretics because she may be at risk for abusing these medications. She may even have a history of laxative or diuretic abuse.

If the recovering athlete has symptoms that are determined to be related to her disorder but are not serious enough to warrant medical intervention, the athlete should be reassured that the problems are not unusual given her history. Additionally, explain to the athlete why the problems appeared, and give her more natural remedies for them. For example, the trainer might tell an athlete who complains of constipation that this problem is not unusual for a person recovering from an eating disorder, and the body may simply need more time to make the necessary adjustments. Inform her that laxatives will slow this adjusting process by the use of unnatural means. Additionally, tell the athlete that the best way to normalize digestion is through normal and natural means such as an increase

in fluid and fiber intake as well as activity or exercise. Similarly, an athlete requesting a diuretic or "water pill" to alleviate bloating or edema might be told that this type of medication only creates a cycle of fluid loss followed by rebound water retention; it tends to maintain (and in many cases exacerbate) the problem it is being used to remedy. A reasonable recommendation would be for the athlete to moderately reduce salt intake while ingesting normal amounts of fluid to allow the body to regulate itself—a process that may take days or longer. Proper management of these situations requires that the sport-related staff know how the body works, how various symptoms may be related to an eating disorder, and how best to dispense this information. This again emphasizes the commitment that the sport staff must make if it is to provide optimal management.

Many gastrointestinal (GI) complications of hospitalized patients suffering from anorexia nervosa can be effectively treated with conservative GI management, psychiatric care, and educational methods (Waldholtz & Andersen, 1990). If these patients' GI symptoms can be managed conservatively, then a general rule for management following successful treatment is that time, weight restoration, and normalized eating are better methods than medical intervention unless a specific medical condition warrants the immediate use of medication. Whenever sport-related personnel are unsure about whether a medication or treatment is appropriate for the athlete who has had an eating disorder, they should consult a specialist in the treatment of eating disorders, preferably the health care professionals providing the athlete's treatment.

Another situation involving medication that may need special management with a recovering athlete concerns medications that may inadvertently depress the athlete or negatively affect his or her gastrointestinal tract or appetite. Such effects could possibly result in a recurrence of eating-disorder symptoms. An example of this type of drug is anti-inflammatory medication sometimes prescribed for sport-related injuries. Athletes with an eating disorder who require such medication should be closely monitored for these effects. If they do occur, the physician working with the athlete should substitute an alternative anti-inflammatory agent. Relatedly, the medical and support staff should be aware that some athletes may abuse these medications, especially those who use them to ease the discomfort associated with overuse injuries. We have also seen athletes abuse these medications to reduce appetite or induce nausea to restrict their food intake.

Assessing Medication and Symptoms

Sport-related staff need to know about medications and how the body works to properly manage situations involving medication decisions; they also need to know how the athlete's symptoms may be related to an eating disorder, what information they need to give the athlete, and how best to dispense this information.

Special Sport Issues

Throughout this chapter, we have described sport issues that the sport management team will have to address. Turning now in a slightly different direction, we examine special sport circumstances that may affect the athlete with an eating disorder. Intuitively, overtraining, staleness, and injury appear to present additional risk factors for an athlete predisposed to develop an eating disorder. Although most researchers in the eating-disorder field have previously overlooked these special sport circumstances, we believe that they warrant further examination because they may present additional challenges to the sport management team.

Overtraining and Staleness

A relatively new area of research in sport performance involves overtraining and its apparent effects on performance. More important for our purposes here, it also probably relates to eating disorders. Physical pursuits that require a high degree of aerobic fitness sometimes involve training schedules that progressively increase to a level in excess of routine training aimed at maintaining performance (Raglin, in press). This planned period of intensified training has been commonly referred to as overtraining. A schedule of overtraining is typically followed by a period of reduced training called taper. Some believe that a schedule of overtraining and tapering leads to significant improvements in power and performance. However, Raglin (1990, in press) has examined the effects of overtraining and concludes that overtraining can either worsen or improve performance; the results depend on aspects of the training as well as the characteristics of the athlete.

When overtraining leads to negative effects, it is called staleness. Morgan, Brown, Raglin, O'Connor, and Ellickson (1987) view staleness as a syndrome because it is associated with depression, disturbances in sleep, loss of appetite and weight, reduced libido, and muscle soreness and heaviness. Morgan et al. have pointed out that these symptoms are identical to those of major depression. Although it is not known what causes staleness, Costill et al. (1988) state that nutritional deficiencies may place athletes at greater risk for becoming stale.

One of the self-defeating aspects of staleness is that when performance decreases or reaches a plateau, many athletes respond by training harder. This can result in a vicious cycle in which the athlete exacerbates the condition by continually increasing training in an attempt to overcome a plateau (Raglin, in press).

What do overtraining and staleness have to do with eating disorders? Overtraining appears to be very relevant to the anorexic or bulimic athlete. Many athletes with eating disorders use their own overtraining schedules (actually overexercising) to legitimize or rationalize the use of excessive exercise as a means of weight loss or purgation. They claim, however, that they are exercising to improve their sport performance. In fact, they may be decreasing performance by promoting staleness. If performance declines, then the athlete is apt to train (exercise) even harder. Remember, the individual (athlete in this case) with an eating disorder seldom views herself as good enough. She may overexercise initially in an effort to compensate for not being good enough. She may then train even harder. The athlete with an eating disorder may have already established her own "overtraining" (overexercising) schedule without her coach being aware of it. If the coach then recommends an increase in exercise or an overtraining schedule, the athlete's undernourished body is taxed even further in that a true overtraining schedule requires a significant increase in calories. Raglin suggests that the characteristics of the athlete determine in part whether the effect of overtraining is positive or negative. The athlete with an eating disorder is not likely to comply with the increased caloric demands of overtraining. Consequently, the overtraining process is not apt to produce positive results. Additionally, the athlete may be more at risk medically without adequate nutrition. She may also be more at risk psychologically when she is unable to produce the desired results from the overtraining regimen.

Overtraining is also relevant to the athlete with an eating disorder in terms of the depressive symptoms associated with it. Many individuals with eating disorders are depressed. Overtraining may maintain or exacerbate depressive symptoms in athletes with eating disorders. Depression can have only a negative effect on sport performance. Unfortunately, based on what we know about overtraining and the athlete with an eating disorder, we again predict that the athlete will train even harder when performance decreases, which in essence places her at even greater risk.

Because staleness may be due to nutritional factors, it is probably safe to assume that the athlete with an eating disorder is more at risk to develop staleness. As staleness negatively affects sport performance, we again expect the athlete to increase her exercise, thereby increasing her risk. The fact that staleness can lead to loss of appetite and weight obviously makes her risk even greater.

From the standpoint of proper management of the athlete with an eating disorder, overtraining is obviously not a beneficial training method for an athlete in treatment, and it may not be appropriate for many athletes who have successfully completed treatment. Even though we know very little at this point about the use of overtraining with at-risk athletes, the possible positive outcomes in terms of sport performance do not outweigh the more probable risks. Additionally, we can use what we do know about overtraining and staleness to help sport support staff, as well as the athlete, understand why it is important that the athlete with an eating disorder not exercise excessively, regardless of her stage in treatment.

Injury

The injured athlete presents a special set of challenges to the management team. Injury can precipitate an eating disorder in the predisposed athlete and can also hamper treatment and aftercare in the athlete with an existing disorder. The role injury may play in precipitating an eating disorder was briefly mentioned in an earlier chapter. Andersen (1990) reported that many males with eating disorders begin their symptoms following a sport injury. This may be one area in which males are more at risk than females, although many female athletes may also be at increased risk following injury.

In addition, among athletes who are predisposed to develop an eating disorder, injured athletes may be more at risk for such development than their uninjured counterparts, for several reasons. An injury tends to curtail the athlete's exercise and training. As a result, the athlete may gain weight due to less energy expenditure. Or, even if weight gain does not occur, the athlete may develop an irrational fear of weight gain. In either case, the athlete may begin to diet as a means of compensating.

Injured athletes are also likely to become depressed. If they are predisposed to have an eating disorder, this depression can play a role in the development of the disorder in at least two ways. First, depression often changes a person's eating patterns by increasing or decreasing appetite and caloric intake. Second, the athlete could use the eating disorder to manage that depression, as we described in earlier chapters.

The sport management team should be aware that in some athletes, frequent, recurrent, or overuse injuries may signal the presence of an emotional problem that involves an eating disturbance. This information is important in identifying the athlete with an eating disorder, and it can also be very important in managing the athlete once a disorder has been detected. Anxiety and depression—symptoms characteristic of many individuals with eating disorders—may increase an athlete's risk of injury due to his or her lowered psychological and physical resistance and reduced concentration. This is one reason that some athletes with eating disorders should not train or compete while symptomatic. It is also why the sport management team must very closely monitor the athlete who is still training or competing while in treatment.

Conclusion

For a variety of reasons, we believe that athletes with an eating disorder should not train or compete until cleared by the health care professionals providing their treatment. In cases where competition or limited training is permissible, careful consideration must ensure that the athletes allowed to participate will not increase their medical or psychological risks by doing so. Preferably, this would include athletes for whom training or competition can be helpful in terms of motivation. Once selected, these athletes must then be closely monitored for any deleterious effects. Decisions as to whether the athlete may continue with training or competition are not to be based on sport considerations but are to be determined solely on their effect on the athlete's treatment. Most important, an athlete's treatment must never be subordinated to his or her sport.

Managing the athlete with an eating disorder before, during, and following treatment can be a very challenging and complex process. Working effectively in this regard requires a significant commitment of the sport management team's time, effort, and perhaps even money. More specifically, coaches, athletic trainers, team physicians, and other members of the sport management team need a working knowledge of eating disorders. They may have to be trained to know when and how to respond. They may need to change some of their typical management behaviors that are inconsistent with working effectively with the athlete with an eating disorder. Relatedly, members of the sport support staff need to involve themselves in efforts to reduce the risk to athletes through preventive strategies and programming. In the next chapter, we will look at some possibilities in this area.

CHAPTER 7

Education and Prevention

To this point, we have been concerned primarily with early identification and treatment of athletes who either have an eating disorder or are at risk for developing one. This approach to management involves dealing with the problem after it has developed. This is called remediation or, more positively, secondary prevention. Through secondary prevention, we attempt to shorten the duration of the disorder through early identification and intervention. We would also like to consider the possibility of primary prevention, which means attempting to preclude the development of the problem.

Ideally, a primary preventive approach to addressing the problem of eating disorders in athletes involves the development of educational information and programs that deter athletes from developing an eating disorder. More specifically, the goal would be to inoculate individuals (athletes) against the factors that predispose them to become eating disordered. Although this is the goal of many prevention programs, there is unfortunately no simple way to accomplish it.

If we begin our preventive efforts with a look at predisposing factors, we quickly find that our options are limited. Certainly we have little or no control over individual, biological, and familial factors. This leaves only sociocultural factors as a possibility. It would seem reasonable to begin our preventive efforts in this area, given that dieting is inextricably tied to society's emphasis on and misconceptions about being thin, and given that dieting is the primary precursor or precipitant to the development of eating disorders. Somehow we must lessen the importance that society places on thinness to remove dieting as the precipitant to the development of these disorders.

It is probably naive to think that we can easily change the sociocultural influences about thinness. This is a somewhat pessimistic and doubtful attitude shared by others (Hsu, 1990; Vandereycken & Meermann, 1984). However, if we reduce the scope of our goals to the sport environment rather than society at large, then perhaps we have reason to feel more optimistic. Even though we probably cannot prevent athletes from being predisposed to develop eating disorders, we nonetheless believe that athletic departments, coaches, and other sport-related personnel can take several steps to decrease the risk that eating disorders develop within the sport environment. In this chapter, we will discuss educational and preventive strategies in this regard, as well as current aspects of what appears to be a model program.

Educating the Athlete

The pessimism that has sometimes been associated with preventive efforts has also included attempts at educating the target or at-risk population. Hsu (1990) contends that we cannot assume that giving individuals educational information about eating disorders will result in preventing them. In fact, he suggests that educational programming may actually encourage eating disorders by making individuals aware of pathogenic behaviors. Similarly, Garner (1985) suggests that programs aimed at prevention may inadvertently glamorize eating disorders. He noted, however, that we should not construe this as an indictment of prevention efforts but rather should consider it a caution when providing information on eating disorders.

One possible way to avoid the problem that Hsu and Garner discussed is to focus less on eating disorders per se and more on information specifically related to sports, such as nutrition, body weight, body composition, and sport performance. Specific information on eating disorders is still very important, but it is needed more by and is more pertinent to sport-related personnel who work with athletes rather than the athletes themselves.

Educational Programming for Athletes

We are continually amazed at how many myths and misconceptions abound regarding weight, weight loss, body composition, and sport performance as well as the relationships that are believed to exist between these factors. Thus, our primary educational concern in this regard is to provide accurate information about these and other factors in the sport environment in an effort to reduce the misinformation that may lead athletes to engage in behaviors that are unhealthy, unhelpful, or even counterproductive.

Nutrition and Eating.   In no area have our patients with eating disorders been more misinformed than in nutrition. Typically, they know the number of calories or the percentage of fat in every food they eat (and often overestimate these), but they have little or no idea about what the body needs to be healthy and to perform at its best. Myths regarding ideal weight, body fat, and nutrition only increase the chance that an individual might develop an eating disorder. Therefore, we strongly advise that athletes be given accurate and complete information about their nutritional needs. There are several ways that they can receive this information. Before we present these, however, it might be helpful to discuss briefly the lack of accurate nutritional information we often see in our patients.

Some individuals, athletes included, see food as something that they should avoid and believe that "less is better." They often fail to understand the body's need for nutrients and how nutrition helps sustain life and provide energy for everyday functioning.

Individuals at risk for developing eating disturbances usually avoid meat and dairy foods, which means that their regimens are often deficient in necessary fats, protein, calcium, and iron. Protein is vital in building and repairing tissue and maintaining adequate immune system functioning. Because many athletes avoid meat and dairy products, they are at risk for ingesting inadequate amounts of protein. Interestingly, however, these individuals are usually interested in "turning fat to muscle." They assume that by reducing fat they are building lean muscle tissue. They seem unaware that protein is necessary for this process.

If they are also restricting their caloric intake by dieting, they may be getting inadequate amounts of complex carbohydrates—the best energy source. With inadequate carbohydrate and fat intake, the body diverts proteins for use as energy. Proteins are not particularly good energy sources, and using them for energy robs the body of the amino acids necessary for several crucial body functions, such as building muscle tissue.

It is possible for someone to get adequate amounts of protein without eating meat, but it requires more effort and time than many busy athletes are willing to make in the way of food shopping, meal planning, and preparation. Avoiding meats also puts an individual at risk for iron deficiency. Too little iron can cause anemia, which results in complaints of tiredness and weakness. Eating-disordered individuals—athletes included—seem unable to make the connection between feeling weak or tired and the lack of carbohydrates and iron-containing foods in their diets.

As expected, fat is the most avoided nutrient. It is so taboo among many of our patients that we refer to it as the "F word." Actually, fats are an important food source, and most dietitians recommend that we get 30% of our calories from them, especially the mono- and polyunsaturated fats. Athletes, however, can go as low as 20% because of increased carbohydrates. The body needs dietary fat for absorbing fat-soluble vitamins as well as for aiding in digestion. This need for dietary fat is evidenced by the high cholesterol levels of many of our anorexic patients. Typically, this does not represent true hypercholesterolemia. It is believed that depriving the body of dietary fat causes it to provide fat in the only way it can—through increasing cholesterol. When the patient increases dietary fat intake to a more normal level, his or her serum cholesterol usually returns to a lower, healthier level. Uninformed weight-conscious individuals often criticize fat because they think calories from fat burn more slowly than calories from other food sources. Actually, fats provide a more concentrated source of energy; 1 gram of fat equals 9 calories, as compared to 4 calories for 1 gram of protein or carbohydrate. Relatedly, fats provide a sense of satiety longer than other food sources. For this reason, fat has sometimes been referred to as the "satiety nutrient" (Boutacoff, Zollman, & Mitchell, 1987).

Fat is probably the most misunderstood of all food sources and thus has more eating and weight myths and misconceptions associated with it. For example, dietary fat is often incorrectly assumed to be the same as body fat. Also, people often think all fats are unhealthy and are to be avoided, regardless of whether they are saturated or unsaturated.

As we mentioned previously, many dieters or athletes often avoid dairy products because they believe they are too high in fat and will cause weight gain. When informed that skim milk has no fat, they still resist including it in their regimens. Just as these individuals appear unaware of their need for protein for building muscle tissue, they seem equally unaware of the skeletal system's need for calcium. They appear to be oblivious to the relationship between inadequate ingestion of calcium and stress fractures, bone and joint pain, bone density loss, and potentially osteoporosis. When calcium intake is inadequate, the body attempts to compensate by drawing calcium from the skeleton, leading to heightened risk of fractures and osteoporosis. As we discussed in chapter 4, this situation is exacerbated in the individual who is so thin that she is amenorrheic.

Finally, many weight-conscious individuals are apparently unaware of the body's need to be properly hydrated. They like that they weigh less when dehydrated. When someone explains to them that the weight loss is actually just fluid loss, many say they don't care; they're interested only in what the scale says. To them, weight is weight and the less of it, the better. They are either unaware or unperturbed that dehydration removes fluids that are necessary for good health and also removes electrolytes that are vital for proper functioning of all of the body's major systems. Individuals with eating disorders usually resist trading dehydration and decreased weight for improved health and possible weight gain.

Based on the previous discussion, it should be obvious that athletes need accurate nutritional information. How should this information be presented? We have several recommendations in this regard. First, when feasible, each athlete should see a dietitian for a nutritional assessment at the beginning, middle, and end of each season to determine whether her regimen meets the nutritional needs of her body and sport. This also provides an excellent opportunity for identifying an athlete who has an eating disorder or is at risk for developing anorexia nervosa or bulimia nervosa. The dietitian is probably the individual best qualified to provide the athlete with a nutritional assessment, an individualized meal plan, and nutritional information to increase existing knowledge as well as to dispel unhelpful myths about eating and weight. A dietitian or qualified sport personnel should offer team members nutritional information on a regular basis to maintain their awareness at an appropriate level and to communicate that sport personnel value proper nutrition as a way to ensure their athletes' good health. In addition, a mental health practitioner or the team's psychologist (if it has one) who is knowledgeable about eating disorders should talk with the team at least once each season to alert everyone to early signs of eating disturbances. Information in a variety of media forms dealing with nutrition, eating, and eating disorders should be available in a readily accessible location for the athlete's private perusal and study. In this regard, the NCAA (1989) has produced some excellent written and videotape materials. Finally, it should be communicated to athletes that the sport management team is following the previous recommendations to ensure their health. This lets the athletes know that their health rather than their weight or performance is of primary importance.

Dieting.   Probably as much misinformation exists about dieting, especially restrictive dieting, as about nutrition, and for this reason athletes need to be informed of the facts about dieting. Throughout this book we have discussed many of these, the most important being that dieting can precipitate an eating disorder. Also of importance to the athlete considering a diet is that diets do not work for most people—any weight lost tends to be regained; in fact, people may regain more than they lost. Athletes also need to know that dieting can lead to overeating or binge eating, resulting in weight gain and a sense of being unable to control one's eating. Athletes also need to realize the possible health risks involved with dieting, as well as how dieting may affect their sport performance. For these reasons, they should be told not to diet without first discussing it with appropriate medical, psychological, or sport-related personnel.

Body Weight and Composition.   We have discussed these issues previously and will not repeat ourselves here. Suffice it to say, however, that these concepts are used in the sport environment, and as a result athletes need to understand the difference between the two, especially as they relate to strength and scale weight.

Talking with a female athlete about body composition or body fat may be just as disturbing as talking with her about weight. Similarly, measuring body fat may produce the same effect as weighing her. The athlete therefore needs to understand the concept of body composition, but more importantly she needs to understand how and why the measure is being taken and how the information will be used to benefit her. She also needs information about how body composition and weight are related to menstrual functioning and overall health. Some female athletes don't know why men's body fat levels are usually lower than theirs despite similar training regimens. They must understand why females cannot attain and maintain the same body fat levels as males and be healthy and perform well athletically. Male athletes need to understand that at some point continued weight loss reaches the point of diminishing returns and is apt to result in loss of fluid and lean tissue. For this reason, an athlete may perform worse at 5% body fat than he did at 7%.

Sport Performance.   It is important that athletes understand the components that contribute to sport performance. Certainly, physical factors play a significant role, and there are probably no substitutes for fitness, strength, speed, and agility. Body fat composition is another physical factor that can affect sport performance in some athletes. However, it is only one factor. Thus, do not overemphasize the purported relationship between body fat and performance. Instead, encourage athletes to work on more psychological contributing factors, ones that they can perhaps control more than physical factors. In this regard, Orlick (1990) reported that when interviewing some of the world's best athletes, coaches, and scouts about the ingredients necessary to achieve at the highest level in sport, he found disagreement on the physical attributes considered necessary. However, he found almost total agreement on the psychological factors—commitment and self-control. In a similar study with National Hockey League coaches and scouts, Orlick found that "desire, determination, attitude, heart, and self-motivation were most often mentioned as the crucial ingredients that tilted the balance between making it and not making it at the professional level" (p. 10). Further, the physically talented hockey players in this study who were not successful were found to be deficient in commitment or to be unable to cope with stress on and off the ice. Orlick's findings lend credence to the notion presented earlier that physical attributes probably establish a ceiling on sport performance, whereas psychological factors determine how close to that ceiling the athlete is able to achieve.

The athlete who is too focused on body fat composition and how it relates to performance might be reminded that major achievements in sport occurred before the concept of body fat composition was applied to sport and even before it was formulated. An excellent example comes from Roger Bannister, who ran the first sub-4-minute mile in 1954. When recently asked about his body fat composition at the height of his running career, Dr. Bannister remarked that body fat composition was not done at the time he was an athlete (R.G. Bannister, personal communication, October 29, 1991).

Education and Training
for Sport-Related Personnel

Many coaches and other support staff need to be exposed to several areas of education and training, but we can probably collapse these into four general areas. The first two involve what we have tried to provide in this book—information about the identification, understanding, and management of eating disorders in athletes as well as information about sport-related factors that may be related to the development of eating disorders. The third involves health-related issues such as nutrition, dieting, and menstrual functioning. The fourth concerns raising the consciousness of male sport support staff regarding issues specific to female athletes.

Eating Disorders.   It is clear that many coaches and other sport personnel need basic information about eating disorders. It is equally clear that many of these individuals often play either a direct or indirect role in their athlete's disordered eating. Not only do they need a better understanding of these disorders, but more importantly they need to be aware of their role in them. This is evidenced by some coaches embracing suboptimal weights and pathogenic weight control measures (actually anorexic or bulimic symptoms) in an attempt to enhance an athlete's performance. What is even more perplexing is that they are promoting these measures despite research indicating that the complications of these practices tend to decrease performance. Why is this occurring? There are probably several reasons, but a general answer is that these sport-related individuals are often misinformed or uninformed about nutrition, unhealthy eating practices, pathogenic weight loss methods, and eating disorders and their relationships to sport performance.

A more specific answer to the preceding question probably relates to Hsu's (1990) contention that the societal values contributing to the development of eating disorders are not apt to change as a result of scientifically based information. He contends that these values are more "spiritual" and thus are not subject to change based on information that is scientific. A similar phenomenon may be operating in the sport environment; aspects of that environment that contribute to the development of eating disorders in athletes (e.g., the purported relationship between body composition and performance) may be based on half-truths that have been exaggerated or overgeneralized. For example, many individuals in the world of sport steadfastly believe that a leaner athlete performs better than an athlete with a higher percent of body fat. However, when asked where they obtained this information, most do not cite relevant literature. Instead, they respond that they just "know" it from their experience. This is not to suggest that coaches necessarily should be able to cite experimental literature or that we should make sport more "scientific." It may mean, however, that the values these individuals hold may not be very changeable, regardless of factual data to the contrary. Nonetheless, it is important that these data be made available to sport-related personnel in a manner that facilitates their understanding and appropriate application. Again, our recommendation is not to make sport more scientific, but to make it safer, healthier, and more enjoyable for athletes while allowing them an opportunity to perform closer to their potential. Thus, when relevant scientific data are available, sport personnel will benefit by applying it in as objective and judicious a manner as possible to those athletes for whom it is most appropriate. This may require considerable open-mindedness from some in the sport community.

Because we are talking about changing beliefs and attitudes that are based in part on personal experience, the kind of open-mindedness necessary for change may require training that is more experiential in nature. Such an approach to training and educating sport personnel has been proposed and implemented by Sesan (1989). In addition to providing the more traditional information on eating disorders for these individuals, Sesan added an experiential component in which sport personnel explore their own values and attitudes about weight, dieting, and body image. More important, they are made aware of how they might communicate their values and attitudes to their athletes.

Experiential training has considerable potential for the education of sport personnel, particularly with respect to beliefs and values based on their personal experience. The potential benefit of such training is not in question; the question is whether sport-related personnel, especially males, will avail themselves of this potential. We have talked about the commitment of time, effort, and resources these individuals need to make in the management and prevention of eating disorders. This type of training requires a personal commitment—one that is difficult for many individuals to make. This difficulty is often related to the person's fear or apprehension rather than simply to his opposition or unwillingness. Perhaps this fear and apprehension could be lessened for male participants if an appropriate male professional provided the necessary training; the team psychologist would be an ideal choice.

Nutrition.   Many coaches are probably similar to many of their athletes in that they believe they have a sufficient knowledge of nutrition and how it relates to sport performance. In reality, many often operate from a system of nutrition based on anecdotal information and their own eating experiences and those of successful athletes they have coached, as well as common myths and misconceptions about eating, weight, and weight loss. A study by Wolf, Wirth, and Lohman (1979) that looked at the nutritional practices of collegiate coaches indicated a need for more information about nutrition. Although this is an older study and we hope that coaches are now better informed, we cannot afford to make that assumption. The same nutritional education we recommend for athletes is probably appropriate for most coaches and other sport-related personnel. This type of educational information is probably best provided by a dietitian experienced in working with athletes.

Menstrual Functioning.   The menstrual functioning of athletes is another area in which sport-related individuals need more information. In our experience, many of these individuals seldom inquire about their athletes' menstrual status; this is particularly true of many male coaches. Many are unaware that the weights or body fat levels they recommend to their athletes will not allow for normal menstrual functioning. Many do not know that amenorrhea can lead to skeletal system injuries and difficulties; they still accept amenorrhea as a normal part of being an athlete. Relatedly, Wilson, Abdenour, and Keye (1991) suggest that menstrual disorders may interfere with sport performance and that coaches and trainers (in addition to their athletes) are often unaware of the medical basis and treatments of these disorders. Because amenorrhea or irregular menses is a typical symptom of eating disorders, it is imperative that coaches and athletic trainers be aware of their athletes' menstrual status and understand its implications for their health, treatment, and sport performance. Equally important, many athletes are not likely to discuss menstrual problems with their male coaches. This makes it important for coaches and trainers to become more comfortable talking with their athletes about this subject and recommending a gynecological examination when warranted. The team physician might be the best person to provide the necessary education and training in this area.

Raising Consciousness.   Many male coaches and other sport support personnel need to know more about women's issues that relate directly or indirectly to eating disorders. Most importantly, this involves why weight is such a sensitive and personal issue for many women. Many men don't realize the pressures women feel regarding their weight; they are unaware that many women associate thinness with success, attractiveness, and happiness or, more negatively, that a lack of thinness is sometimes synonymous with failure, unattractiveness, and unhappiness. Because weight is such an emotionally charged issue for many women, male coaches and other male staff must eliminate derogatory comments or behaviors about weight. These comments and behaviors are sometimes blatant, such as when weights are posted for all to see and the heaviest person, the person who has gained weight, or the person in need of weight loss is designated in some fashion. Evidently, some uninformed coaches use such degrading strategies to "motivate" athletes.

Blatant offenses are relatively easy to see and obviously need elimination. So do more subtle comments or behaviors that some coaches may not realize are inappropriate or offensive. Male coaches are sometimes surprised to learn that what they consider innocuous comments are perceived by a female athlete as rude and embarrassing—comments like "You're carrying a little extra baggage." Or they may make comments while engaging in what they consider innocent touching, such as pinching "fat" around the athlete's waist. Coaches must realize that the athlete is not being too sensitive if she responds negatively to such behaviors or comments; rather, the coach is being too insensitive.

The effect of this type of inappropriate behavior is further complicated by the importance that athletes often assign to their coaches. A good athlete very much needs and wants to please her coach. Any message from a coach, especially a head coach, carries considerable significance. Negative messages are no exception and can greatly affect any athlete. Unfortunately, the individual likely to be most affected by these messages is one with low self-esteem, such as a person who is predisposed to develop an eating disorder. These issues are very real for women, and the sport personnel must deal with them sensitively and respectfully.

This raising of consciousness is related to the larger issue of males coaching female athletes. Certainly, there are excellent male coaches of women. However, most of the women athletes with eating disorders we've worked with have been coached by males. It is difficult to discern what this means. Our only data in this regard are anecdotal, so it is probably premature to even suggest that a relationship exists between the development of eating disorders in female athletes and factors related to their male coaches. It may simply be because more coaches are male. In terms of educating coaches, this means we may need an educative approach geared specifically to males. This is further evidenced by findings in our clinical practice (again anecdotal data) that males (i.e., fathers, husbands, boyfriends, brothers, etc.) appear to have greater difficulty understanding an eating disorder, especially how and why it develops. We have also found, however, that once they understand the disorder, significant males are often immensely helpful to the affected individual in overcoming it.

Recommended Educational Materials

Our purpose in writing this book was to give members of the sport community a practical guide to managing athletes with eating disorders. Although we believe the information contained in this book can be helpful in this regard, we view it as a beginning. Based on our own work with individuals with eating disorders, we have found that one cannot know too much; usually we do not know enough. For this reason, we have included a list of materials in Appendix A that we believe can significantly supplement the contents of this book. We have divided that list by general content area.

Preventing Eating Disorders

Besides educational efforts aimed at athletes and those who manage them, several strategies might be employed in an effort to prevent the development of eating disorders in athletes. Our focus in this section will be on preventive strategies relating to attitudes and practices that too often are an accepted part of the sport environment.

Deemphasize Weight

The simplest way to deemphasize weight is not to weigh athletes or not to stress weight by commenting on it. At the very least, it should not be emphasized more than other factors. Actually, there are several ways to deemphasize weight. Most important, emphasize the person rather than the person's body. As we have discussed previously, probably several components interact to produce quality sport performance. Certainly, the individual's physical abilities and attributes should not be underestimated. But instead of emphasizing weight or body fat composition in the physical realm, we might more appropriately focus on physical conditioning and strength development. As one coach remarked, "I don't care how much an athlete weighs if she's strong enough and fit enough to do what I want her to do." If the focus must be on enhancing speed or quickness, first pursue training strategies other than weight loss.

We can also deemphasize body size, shape, weight, or fat composition by placing more emphasis on the mental and emotional components of performance. Not only does considerable potential for enhanced performance exist in these two areas, but an individual who improves her mental and emotional capacities is in no way placed at risk. The same claim obviously cannot be made for weight loss or a decrease in body fat.

Eliminate Group Weigh-Ins

We oppose indiscriminant weighing of individuals for a variety of reasons. We especially oppose group weigh-ins. Based on reports from coaches, athletic trainers, and athletes, group weigh-ins are apparently common in the sport environment. For an individual with an eating disorder, a group weigh-in can constitute almost public degradation. She is often ashamed of her body and assumes that she is too fat, regardless of her actual size, shape, and weight. Public weighings are apt to make her anxious and angry. If she knows when they are to take place, she may not eat for days beforehand or may use a variety of purgation or dehydration techniques to ensure that her weight is "low enough." Even for the female athlete who is not eating disordered, public weigh-ins can create considerable psychological discomfort.

What is the purpose of a group weigh-in? If there is a legitimate reason for weighing an athlete, weigh her privately. The individual athlete is not the only concern, however. We believe that group weigh-ins may create more competitiveness among women athletes with regard to thinness. One female athlete gave this report on her experience with team weigh-ins: "There was no way I was going to be the heaviest—I'd do whatever I had to not to have the highest weight." This competitiveness may increase the likelihood that particular individuals resort to pathologic means of controlling weight.

Sometimes the negative effects of weighing can be attenuated if the athlete is given a legitimate reason why she is being weighed. Athletes suggest to us that they are more anxious when no one tells them why they are being weighed and what is to be done with the results.

Any coach or athletic trainer who routinely weighs athletes either publicly or privately should seriously consider why weighing is necessary. If it cannot be determined that this information is helpful in some regard or if it is not going to be used to benefit the athlete, then weighing—especially group weighing—should be avoided. The risk that it will cause discomfort or problems for the athlete is too great.

In many ways, body fat measurements may create the same turmoil and difficulty as weighing, so the same cautions apply to measuring body fat composition. If weight or body fat measures have to be taken, we recommend that it be done at the beginning and end of the season. Inform the athletes when this is to occur and what the results will be used for. Of course, these measurements should also be taken privately. Finally, we also advise asking the athlete whether she wants to know her weight and body fat composition. Some may feel more comfortable not knowing. For those who do not want to know their weight, simply have them face away from the scale when they are being weighed.

Eliminate Unhealthy "Subcultural" Aspects

Sometimes the pathogenic weight loss measures that athletes use have almost become an accepted part of their sport. As a result, some athletes assume such measures are acceptable and even value them as part of the "subculture" of their sport. The epitome of this type of thinking occurs in wrestling. Some wrestlers seem to view the dehydrating techniques they use as a sign of toughness that sets them apart from other athletes. Contributing to these attitudes is the athletes' assumption that because these methods are so accepted in their sport, their opponents are using them as well. One wrestler reported that he needed to lose 7 pounds before a weigh-in for an upcoming match in only 5 days. When asked how he would be able to have the necessary strength and stamina to wrestle after his quick weight loss, he smiled and said, "The other guy will have done the same thing, so it all evens out."

Coaches can play an important role in changing these attitudes and behaviors that have more to do with tradition, myth, and subculture than with factual information relating to sport performance. Sometimes athletes assume that their coaches are aware of some of the potentially unhealthy behaviors they are engaging in, and because the coach has not specifically directed them to stop, he is condoning their use. Coaches need to be very clear and direct about the acceptability of training strategies and techniques. They can communicate this clarity and directiveness in many ways, but the most important is the coach's response when he or she finds out that an athlete is engaging in pathogenic weight-control behaviors. We recommend the firm but gentle approach in such instances. The coach needs to be aware that most athletes are simply trying to improve their performance and will try almost anything to accomplish that goal. The coach should commend the athlete for his attitude and commitment, but should firmly tell him that the behaviors are unhelpful and unhealthy and are therefore unacceptable.

Treat Each Athlete Individually

When it comes to our expectations for someone—an athlete in this case—we tend to base our expectations or goals for that person on our experiences with others or ourselves in similar situations. Or we may base them on what we have been told or have read. In essence, we often take general or aggregate information and apply it to specific individuals. This application is relevant and appropriate to some individuals. However, for others this application fits less well or perhaps not at all. Thus, we must be careful and judicious in applying our general principles to individuals. Practically, this means we must temper our expectations to account for individual differences. This is true when we are working with any aspect of an individual, but it is even more important when we are concerned with an aspect of an individual that is largely out of the individual's control. Weight and weight loss are prime examples. An individual's weight is determined largely by genetics, and this does not change, no matter how many well-known coaches tell us in their commercials, "If I can lose weight, so can you." Some individuals are not able to lose weight. Many who lose weight are unable to maintain that loss. Similarly, a profile of elite athletes in a particular sport that indicates they have a certain percent body fat does not mean that all athletes in that sport can or should strive for the same body composition.

Our discussion of individual differences to this point has focused on the individual's physiological aspects. Equally important are the more psychological or emotional aspects. As different as individuals may be physiologically, even more room for individuality exists in the psychological realm. As such, we are even less able to predict how an individual will respond to a particular set of circumstances. We are working not only with a body, an athlete, or that athlete's performance, but with a whole person—an individual with a unique set of life experiences. By attending to that uniqueness, we are less likely to set up inappropriate or unrealistic expectations for the individual, whether those expectations relate to weight, weight loss, sport performance, or any other aspect of the person that interests us.

A final comment on the need to focus on the athlete's individuality concerns what appears to be a movement to make sport more "scientific." We are now able to condition and train an athlete, as well as monitor his or her performance, using a variety of biomedical approaches and technological gadgets that scientists have developed and refined in recent years. Certainly there is nothing wrong with applying these scientific advances to sport. However, we need to remember that we are still working with a person. We can quantify and measure certain aspects of the athlete's body and performance. This can tell us what's going on inside the body, but it may not come close to telling us what's going on inside the person. As the excellent message from Nike suggests in Figure 7.1, the numbers do not always add up. The individual person does not always "fit" a scientific principle; she cannot be easily quantified. She seldom "fits" a diagnostic category. A well-thought-out scientific approach to managing her difficulties is not always helpful. A conceptually based, professionally applied treatment approach does not always produce positive results. Individual factors can and will affect every aspect of the individual's life. We run the risk of overlooking or underestimating the effect of these factors through overgeneralization.

In this book, we have been somewhat guilty of what we just described. We've discussed numerous aspects, issues, and management strategies concerning athletes with eating disorders. In most cases, we have made generalizations—albeit for instructional

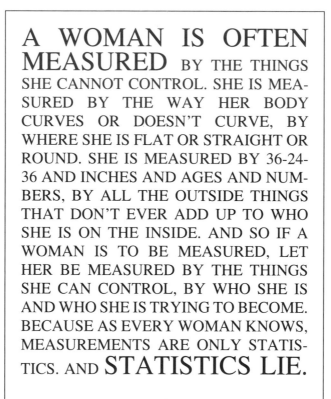

A WOMAN IS OFTEN MEASURED BY THE THINGS SHE CANNOT CONTROL. SHE IS MEASURED BY THE WAY HER BODY CURVES OR DOESN'T CURVE, BY WHERE SHE IS FLAT OR STRAIGHT OR ROUND. SHE IS MEASURED BY 36-24-36 AND INCHES AND AGES AND NUMBERS, BY ALL THE OUTSIDE THINGS THAT DON'T EVER ADD UP TO WHO SHE IS ON THE INSIDE. AND SO IF A WOMAN IS TO BE MEASURED, LET HER BE MEASURED BY THE THINGS SHE CAN CONTROL, BY WHO SHE IS AND WHO SHE IS TRYING TO BECOME. BECAUSE AS EVERY WOMAN KNOWS, MEASUREMENTS ARE ONLY STATISTICS. AND STATISTICS LIE.

Reprinted with permission of NIKE, Inc.

Figure 7.1

purposes—but generalizations nonetheless. Although these were necessary to facilitate the reader's understanding, unfortunately they may have inadvertently moved the focus away from the uniqueness of the individual athlete. Even though most individuals (athletes in this case) with eating disorders share many characteristics, each is nonetheless unique and special. As such, each requires special treatment and management.

Guidelines for Appropriate Weight Loss

In most cases, we do not view weight loss as a viable option for most athletes. This is because weight loss is not a reasonable option for most individuals, whether they're athletes or not. As discussed previously, dieting is not effective; most people cannot lose weight and then maintain the loss. More importantly, it can be risky. A low-calorie diet in particular is unhealthy from a nutritional standpoint and can precipitate an eating disturbance or outright disorder. For these reasons, we recommend that athletes not be asked or encouraged to diet.

Even though our recommendation about not dieting is based on well-established fact, we are not so naive as to believe that dieting will not occur in the sport environment regardless of the problems or risks involved. Consequently, if athletes are going to diet, we strongly recommend the following guidelines to minimize possible risks. First, a health care professional should assess the athlete asked to lose weight to confirm that she is at little or no risk of developing an eating disorder as a result of dieting. This can be done by interviewing the athlete, focusing on her eating and weight history, and assessing any eating disturbance with an instrument such as an eating disorder inventory. Second, the athlete in question should be overweight; that is, her weight should be over her (medically) recommended body weight. Ideally, she should agree with the decision to lose weight. In addition, a dietitian should determine and monitor the weight loss procedure. More specifically, the dietitian should determine a healthy weight range for the particular athlete as well as a meal plan designed to move the athlete gradually into that range. The dietitian should also report any suspected physiological or psychological difficulties to the appropriate health care professional during the weight loss process. Finally, the athlete's sport performance should be closely monitored during the weight loss process to determine if it is in fact increasing as weight and body fat are decreasing. If performance does not significantly increase or actually decreases after a reasonable time, there is no need to continue the athlete's weight loss program for performance reasons. Even if performance does increase as a result of weight loss, the loss is not to exceed the healthy weight range that the dietitian has established. Although the goal of losing weight in this circumstance is to enhance sport performance, everyone involved must remember that the athlete's health is still the first priority, regardless of how successful the weight loss process is in enhancing performance.

Some coaches might argue that they are seeking a change in the athlete's body composition rather than weight loss. This is a very complex issue, and a thorough discussion is beyond the scope of this book. Suffice it to say that from a physiological point of view, it is difficult to affect body composition without affecting body weight; in other words, an athlete who loses body fat is also likely to lose weight. From a psychological point of view, the athlete still tends to perceive the process of increasing lean muscle mass as losing fat (or weight). As a result, whether the regimen is designed to decrease weight, decrease body fat, or increase lean muscle tissue, it probably carries the same risk of precipitating eating disorder symptoms in athletes predisposed to have an eating disorder.

Controlling the Contagion Effect

A contagion effect seems to be associated with some athletes and some sports. This term refers to eating disturbances spreading from one athlete to another. Many athletes learn from their teammates. Unfortunately, what they learn is not always helpful. Learning can take place directly when one athlete tells another that she engaged in a pathogenic weight loss method in an attempt to lose weight. Probably more often learning is vicarious or less direct. An athlete may selectively notice that the top performer in her sport happens to be one of the thinnest, or she may know a successful teammate who diets excessively, uses pathogenic weight loss measures, or trains excessively. Indirect learning may occur as a result of frequent body comparisons made easier by athletes changing clothes and showering together, as well as the revealing sport apparel they wear, such as bathing suits. Or it may occur as an athlete is continually exposed to her teammates' references to and discussions about weight, thinness, and eating, and she begins to believe that these issues really are important.

Unfortunately, we know more about what the contagion effect is and how it operates than we do about how to eliminate it. Eliminating it is probably impossible; trying to control or minimize it will most likely be difficult enough. Obviously, we cannot prevent athletes from making comparisons or talking about weight or thinness. However, if sport personnel deemphasize weight and thinness, perhaps it will be reflected in the athletes' thoughts, attitudes, discussions, and behaviors. We hope that this deemphasis teamed with giving athletes better information on nutrition and health will help control the contagion effect of eating disorders.

Reducing Competitive Thinness

In many ways, competitive thinness has little if anything to do with sport and more to do with the contagion effect just discussed. We know that in the nonathlete population considerable competition exists regarding thinness among women. Many of our patients who are not athletes tell us that when they see another woman who looks thinner, they often feel "fat" and believe that they must lose weight. It is as if only the thinnest woman can be the "winner." When asked what they are competing for or what they expect to win, most are unable to answer. Because nonathlete women participate in this competition, it is probably safe to assume that at least some women athletes also participate in part because they have many of the same needs for thinness. Also, many good athletes are likely to be competitive in any arena. As with the contagion effect, competitive thinness can be reduced if the significant individuals who work with athletes put less emphasis on thinness and give the athletes more helpful information about eating, weight, and performance.

Assistance From Governing Organizations

The individuals who govern amateur and professional sports apparently accept that drug use is dangerous and steps are needed to control it. Many amateur and professional sports now engage in drug testing. Of particular interest in this regard is the acceptance of drug testing for steroid use. This acceptance has occurred even though steroids can make an athlete bigger, stronger, and more aggressive—traits that tend to increase performance in several sports. The importance these governing individuals have assigned to the dangers of steroid use is evidenced by the fact that athletes caught using these substances are usually suspended from competition. Perhaps we need a similar approach to managing dysfunctional eating practices and pathogenic weight control measures in athletes.

By a similar approach, we do not mean a simple medical test like urinalysis to determine the existence of a problem. The development of a procedure by which one can identify disturbed eating is not the impediment to instigating such an approach. The governing bodies of amateur and professional sports must first recognize that eating disorders constitute a potential danger to the athlete—a danger as great as that commonly associated with drug use. To the NCAA's credit, it has developed a very informative series of educational films that deal with eating disorders, nutrition, and measures that coaches and other sport-related personnel can take to manage eating disorders in their athletes (NCAA, 1989). This is an excellent first step that we hope will eventually lead to the type of approach we are advocating.

Providing Education and Treatment: A Model

In an ideal world, all athletes would work with a team of qualified professionals who could provide the type of educational information just described. Additionally, these professionals would be available to work with any athlete identified as having an eating problem or being at risk for developing one. This team approach would involve professionals from a wide range of fields—psychologists, physicians, coaches, dietitians, and athletic trainers, to name just a few. Unfortunately, most very young athletes have only their coaches to rely on. At the high school level, athletic trainers may be involved, but the resources available to the athlete remain limited. In these situations, it is imperative that the coach become as knowledgeable as possible and, at a minimum, find experts in these other fields in the community to call in if and when a problem arises. We realize that resources are often limited in terms of time, money, and expertise. Many who coach young athletes are volunteers or are paid only token salaries. Nevertheless, they have chosen to take on a responsibility that cannot be minimized.

Sports at the collegiate and elite amateur and professional levels probably offer the best opportunity for greater professional support and assistance to a coach and his or her athletes. Although many colleges are also constrained by a lack of funds, we believe that they should make every effort to institute the recommendations outlined in this book, in large part because college-age athletes appear to be a high-risk group. Unfortunately, too few collegiate programs have put energy and resources into this area. One notable exception has been the University of Texas at Austin. After discovering eating problems in some of their female athletes a few years ago, the University of Texas took an active and aggressive approach to instituting educational and remedial programs for all female athletes. Directed by Randa Ryan (1991), the Department of Intercollegiate Athletics for Women has developed a model program, one that we would like to see more colleges and universities follow, as well as other amateur and professional sport groups.

Two aspects of the program at the University of Texas contribute primarily to its success. The first is an impressive team of professionals with a variety of expertise. Eight of the 27 members are physicians with specialties including gynecology, orthopedic surgery, internal medicine, immunology, bone densitometry, and ophthalmology. Additionally, there are specialists in biomechanics, exercise physiology, nutrition, psychology, strength training, pharmacology, body composition, dentistry, and athletic training.

Second, these professionals are involved in an ongoing program of education for athletes and coaches, assessment, referral, and treatment. An example of how the program works involves weight decisions. Nutritionists, athletic trainers, exercise physiologists, and the athletes involved all have input into decisions about the athletes' weight. An appeal process is available to any athlete who is uncomfortable with the recommendation. Also, the program is amenable to modification when necessary. For example, coaches are not currently involved either in weighing the athlete or in decisions regarding weight. This is a recent change in the program's structure; although some people opposed this change initially, most now believe it has been helpful to all concerned.

Figure 7.2 shows the prevention and treatment services available to student-athletes at the University of Texas. Ongoing nutrition programs are available to all athletes, with special programming geared toward incoming freshmen and transfer students. Referrals for treatment can come from the athletes themselves, from coaches, or from other staff members. Treatment options are varied and are determined on an individual basis. Although the University of Texas is not the only university attempting to address the problem of eating disorders in athletes, it does provide an excellent model of a very thorough program that other colleges and universities, as well as amateur and professional sport federations and organizations, might consider implementing.

Key Program Component

In theory, a well-conceived and well-organized program such as the one just described has all the components necessary to function effectively. But will it work in practice? Throughout this book, we have described the importance of the coach and the power he or she has with an athlete. We consider coaches, especially head coaches, the most significant component in the success of a management and prevention program. Athletes may not believe research findings about performance or what psychologists, physicians, or dietitians tell them about their physical or emotional health. More often, however, they believe and do what their coaches tell them. For this

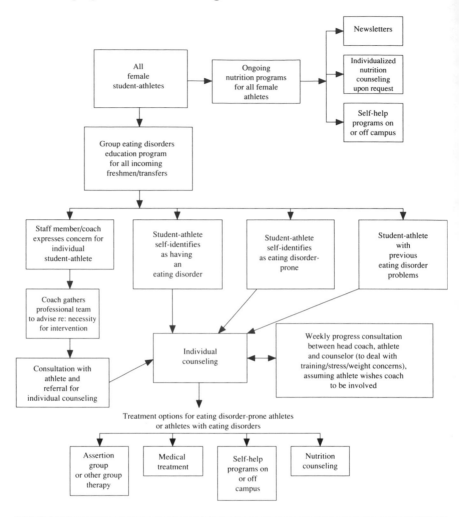

Figure 7.2 Prevention and treatment of eating disorders among student-athletes*

reason, a coach's endorsement of a program is the key component. We have talked about the eating-disordered athlete's fears associated with letting others know of her difficulties and seeking treatment. We have to make it as safe and easy as possible for athletes to come forward and avail themselves of the assistance they need. The coach can be instrumental in this respect. If a coach does not support a program, its survival is in doubt. Without the coach's recommendations and encouragement to use the program, athletes

*Reprinted with permission of Randa Ryan, The Department of Intercollegiate Athletics For Women, University of Texas at Austin.

are less likely to use it, regardless of how well conceived, well organized, or well implemented that program may be.

Conclusion

Educational approaches to the prevention of eating disorders have sometimes been criticized because they may precipitate experimentation with pathogenic weight control measures that can lead to actual disorders. Certainly, some individuals have misused educational information in this manner. In fact, we have worked with patients who began their pathogenic behaviors after watching an educational program or reading materials related to eating disorders. However, it is important to remember that eating disorders are unlikely to occur in individuals who are not predisposed to develop them. Also, an individual whose eating disorder could be precipitated as a result of educational programming was probably enough at risk that any number of factors could or would have eventually precipitated it. We believe that the potential benefit of educational and preventive programs significantly outweighs the relatively small risk involved.

If we are to prevent the development of eating disorders in athletes or at least reduce the risks athletes face, educational programming needs to be aimed at the athletes themselves and must also include the sport-related individuals who manage them. For athletes, the information should emphasize nutrition, eating, dieting, and body weight and composition and how these relate to sport performance. The sport support staff should receive similar information, and we recommend they also be provided with information about identifying and managing eating disorders as well as women's issues that relate to eating disorders. This last issue is particularly important for males who coach female athletes.

We acknowledged that modifying societal values that relate to the development of eating disorders would be helpful but is highly unlikely and suggested that, on a smaller scale, an attempt at prevention should identify aspects of the sport environment that may contribute to the development of such disorders in athletes. We made recommendations about modifying, deemphasizing, or eliminating these aspects or factors in an effort to decrease the risk of eating disorders developing.

Finally, we discussed the components of a model program designed to assist in the secondary and primary prevention of eating disorders in athletes. The key component appears to be the role that coaches play in these programs. Because of the importance that athletes ascribed to their coaches, the success of such programs tends to be related to the commitment and support of the coaches involved.

Epilogue

In this book, we have presented an approach to the management of athletes with eating disorders that bridges the diverse worlds of sports and eating-disorder treatment. Our goal was to educate people involved in the sport environment about eating disorders and how to best manage them, and to increase the awareness of those working in the field of eating disorders about the reality and impor tance of the world of sport. We hope we have answered questions relevant to both worlds. But we also hope this book will raise as many questions as it answers. Clearly, we need more research investigating the apparent relationship between sport participation and the development of eating disorders. In particular, we need to look at factors that may relate to specific sports, training approaches, prevailing attitudes about body composition and performance, and characteristics of coaches and athletes that may increase an athlete's risk of developing a disorder.

Additionally, we have questioned whether athletes as a special population require special approaches to treatment. Do they respond differently to treatment than do their nonathlete counterparts? Will some aspects of traditional treatment be more effective if they are modified for athletes? Presently, we believe that athletes with eating disorder symptoms should not train or compete until the appropriate health care professionals approve such participation. Is this the best way to manage athletes with eating disorders? While writing this book, we posed this question to other practitioners and researchers in the area of eating disorders as well as to individuals from the world of sport. Opinions varied. Some thought it was unconscionable to allow these athletes to compete. Others thought it might hurt their progress in therapy not to allow them to train and compete. Many took a middle-of-the-road position similar to ours, indicating that training and competition may be acceptable in certain circumstances that protect the athlete. Unfortunately, this "specialty" area—a subarea of general eating-disorder treatment—is still young. We have based much of what we recommend and practice on clinical experience and anecdotal information. Obviously, controlled studies investigating various aspects of the treatment of athletes with eating disorders are warranted.

As we conclude this book, we are reminded that people often think athletes are healthier than the general population because of their prowess in sport and their commitment to training and exercise. It is ironic, then, that the same characteristics that contribute to their prowess, along with aspects of their training and exercise, may also contribute to the development of eating disorders in too many athletes. This idea is supported by the research of Moriarty and Moriarty (1991), which suggested that there is cause for concern about eating disorders in fitness instructors. In our clinical experience we have also found this to be true. Again, it is ironic that aerobics or fitness instructors—individuals who most people probably regard as "healthy" and who are responsible for instructing others about fitness and exercise—appear to be a high-risk group for eating disorders. This suggests that for many athletes and other athletically oriented people, "fitness" and "getting in shape" have become synonymous with restrictive dieting, compulsive and obligatory exercise, and eating disorders. Somehow we need to put real "health" back into the eating and exercise regimens of individuals who seem much more concerned about thinness.

Finally, writing one of the first books to address the topic of eating disorders in athletes has both positive and negative aspects. The negative part relates to having little "science" on which to rely. Our knowledge of athletes with eating disorders is still limited and based primarily on clinical experience. For this reason, we can expect that knowledge to change over time. In fact, our own views and practices have changed somewhat in the past 4 to 5 years based on our own experience. Since our earlier articles on the treatment of eating disorders (Thompson & Sherman, 1989) in general, and on athletes and eating disorders (Thompson, 1987) in particular, we have become somewhat more conservative in our thinking and treatment. As a result, we have even made some modifications in our "firm but gentle" approach. We have become firmer, but we hope we haven't changed our gentleness. To sum it all up, those who are the first to jump into a new area of research are probably doomed to make mistakes. As investigations of eating disorders in athletes continue, we will become aware of some of ours. On the positive side, we can stimulate research in this area by providing a basic framework that others can respond to or even react against.

Recommended Reading and Resource Materials

General Information on Eating Disorders

Andersen, A.E. (Ed.) (1990). *Males with eating disorders.* New York: Brunner/Mazel.

Garfinkel, P.E., & Garner, D.M. (1982). *Anorexia nervosa: A multidimensional perspective.* New York: Brunner/Mazel.

Hsu, L.K.G. (1990). *Eating disorders.* New York: Guilford Press.

Johnson, C., & Connors, M. (1987). *The etiology and treatment of bulimia nervosa.* New York: Basic Books.

Mitchell, J.E. (1990). *Bulimia nervosa.* Minneapolis: University of Minnesota Press.

Sherman, R.T., & Thompson, R.A. (1990). *Bulimia: A guide for family and friends.* Lexington, MA: Lexington Books.

Eating Disorders and Athletes

Brownell, K.D., Rodin, J., & Wilmore, J.H. (Eds.) (1991). *Eating, body weight, and performance in athletes: Disorders of modern society.* Philadelphia: Lea & Febiger.

Garner, D.M., & Rosen, L.W. (1991). Eating disorders among athletes: Research and recommendations. *Journal of Applied Sport Science Research, 5,* 100-107.

Grandjean, A.C. (1991). Eating disorders—the role of the athletic trainer. *Athletic Training, 26,* 105-112.

Rosen, L.W., McKeag, D.B., Hough, D.O., & Curley, V. (1986). Pathogenic weight-control behavior in female athletes. *Physician and Sportsmedicine, 14,* 79-86.

Steen, S.N., & Brownell, K.D. (1990). Patterns of weight loss and regain in wrestlers: Has the tradition changed? *Medicine and Science in Sports and Exercise, 22,* 762-768.

Thompson, R.A. (1987). Management of the athlete with an eating disorder: Implications for the sport management team. *The Sport Psychologist, 1,* 114-126.

Educational Resources

Levine, M.P., & Hill, L. (1991). *A 5-day lesson plan on eating disorders: Grades 7-12.* Columbus, OH: The National Anorexic Aid Society. (Printed materials and audiovisual resources.)

National Collegiate Athletic Association. (1989). *Nutrition and eating disorders in college athletics.* Wilkes-Barre, PA: Karol Media. (Videotape and printed materials)

Medical Issues

Drinkwater, B.L., Bruemner, B., & Chesnut, C.H. (1990). Menstrual history as a determinant of current bone density in young athletes. *Journal of the American Medical Association, 263,* 545-548.

Shangold, M., Rebar, R.W., Wentz, A.C., & Schiff, I. (1990). Evaluation and management of menstrual dysfunction in athletes. *Journal of the American Medical Association, 263,* 1665-1669.

Stephenson, J.N. (1991). Medical consequences and complications of anorexia nervosa and bulimia nervosa in female athletes. *Athletic Training, 26,* 130-135.

Sports Nutrition

Clark, N. (1990). *Nancy Clark's sports nutrition guidebook.* Champaign, IL: Leisure Press.

Clark, N., Nelson, M., & Evans, W. (1988). Nutrition education for elite female runners. *Physician and Sportsmedicine, 16,* 124-136.

Eating Disorder Resources

The following organizations provide a variety of information on eating disorders and their treatment. Most provide a list of therapists, physicians, treatment programs, and hospitals specializing in the treatment of eating disorders.

American Anorexia/Bulimia Association, Inc. (AABA)
   133 Cedar Lane
   Teaneck, NJ 07666
   (201) 836-1800
AABA provides a nationwide referral service. It also offers information packets and publishes a newsletter.

Anorexia Nervosa and Associated Disorders (ANAD)
   Box 7
   Highland Park, IL 60035
   (708) 831-3438
ANAD maintains an international referral list of therapists and programs. It also has a newsletter and information packets that it will send on request.

Anorexia Nervosa and Related Eating Disorders, Inc. (ANRED)
   P.O. Box 5102
   Eugene, OR 97405
   (503) 344-1144
ANRED provides a nationwide referral service. In addition, it will send its newsletter and general information packet on request.

National Anorexic Aid Society (NAAS)
   1925 E. Dublin-Granville Road
   Columbus, OH 43229
   (614) 436-1112 or (614) 846-2833
NAAS provides referral services in the United States, Canada, and Great Britain. It also offers a newsletter and additional information on eating disorders.

References

American College of Sports Medicine. (1976). Position stand on weight loss in wrestlers. *Medicine and Science in Sports and Exercise, 8*, xi-xiii.

American Medical Association, Committee on the Medical Aspects of Sports. (1967). Wrestling and weight control. *Journal of the American Medical Association, 201*, 541-543.

American Psychiatric Association. (1987). *Diagnostic and statistical manual of mental disorders* (3rd ed., rev.). Washington, DC: Author.

Andersen, A.E. (1986). Inpatient and outpatient treatment of anorexia nervosa. In K.D. Brownell & J.P. Foreyt (Eds.), *Handbook of eating disorders* (pp. 333-350). New York: Basic Books.

Andersen, A.E. (1988). Anorexia nervosa and bulimia nervosa in males. In D.M. Garner & P.E. Garfinkel (Eds.), *Diagnostic issues in anorexia nervosa and bulimia nervosa* (pp. 166-205). New York: Brunner/Mazel.

Andersen, A.E. (1990). Diagnosis and treatment of males with eating disorders. In A.E. Andersen (Ed.), *Males with eating disorders* (pp. 133-162). New York: Brunner/Mazel.

Andersen, A.E., & Hay, A. (1985). Racial and socioeconomic influences in anorexia nervosa and bulimia. *International Journal of Eating Disorders, 4*, 479-487.

Barrow, G.W., & Sha, S. (1988). Menstrual irregularity and stress fractures in collegiate female distance runners. *American Journal of Sports Medicine, 16*, 209-216.

Benson, J.E., Allemann, Y., Theintz, G.E., & Howald, H. (1990). Eating problems and calorie intake levels in Swiss adolescent athletes. *International Journal of Sports Medicine, 11*, 249-252.

Benson, J.E., Geiger, C.J., Eiserman, P.A., & Wardlaw, G.M. (1989). Relationship between nutrient intake, body mass index, menstrual function, and ballet injury. *Journal of the American Dietetic Association, 89*, 58-63.

Bergstrom, J., & Hultman, E. (1972). Nutrition for maximal sports performance. *Journal of the American Medical Association, 221*, 999-1006.

Black, D.R., & Burckes-Miller, M.E. (1988). Male and female college athletes: Use of anorexia nervosa and bulimia nervosa weight loss methods. *Research Quarterly for Exercise and Sport, 59,* 252-256.

Blumenthal, J.A., O'Toole, L.C., & Chang, J.L. (1984). Is running an analogue of anorexia nervosa? *Journal of the American Medical Association, 252,* 520-523.

Borgen, J.S., & Corbin, C.B. (1987). Eating disorders among female athletes. *Physician and Sportsmedicine, 15,* 89-95.

Boutacoff, L.A., Zollman, M.R., & Mitchell, J.E. (1987). *Healthy eating: A meal planning system* (rev. ed.). Minneapolis: University of Minnesota Press.

Brooks-Gunn, J., Burrow, C., & Warren, M.P. (1988). Attitudes toward eating and body weight in different groups of female adolescent athletes. *International Journal of Eating Disorders, 7,* 749-757.

Brownell, K.D., Steen, S.N., & Wilmore, J.H. (1987). Weight regulation practices in athletes: Analysis of metabolic and health effects. *Medicine and Science in Sports and Exercise, 19,* 546-556.

Burckes-Miller, M.E., & Black, D.R. (1988). Male and female college athletes: Prevalence of anorexia nervosa and bulimia nervosa. *Athletic Training, 23,* 137-140.

Calabrese, L.H., Kirkendall, D.T., Floyd, M., Rapoport, S., Williams, G.W., Weiker, G.G., & Bergfeld, J.A. (1983). Menstrual abnormalities, nutritional patterns and body composition in female classical ballet dancers. *Physician and Sportsmedicine, 11,* 86-98.

Clark, N., Nelson, M., & Evans, W. (1988). Nutrition education for elite female runners. *Physician and Sportsmedicine, 16,* 124-136.

Coleman, E. (1986). Good nutrition and female gymnasts. *Sports Medicine Digest, 8,* 6.

Costar, E.D. (1983, November). Eating disorders: Gymnasts at risk. *International Gymnast,* pp. 58-59.

Costill, D.L., Flynn, M.G., Kirwan, J.P., Houmard, J.A., Mitchell, J.B., Thomas, R., & Park, S.H. (1988). Effects of repeated days of intensified training on muscle glycogen and swimming performance. *Medicine and Science in Sports and Exercise, 20,* 249-254.

Crisp, A.H., & Burns, T. (1990). Primary anorexia nervosa in the male and female: A comparison of clinical features and prognosis. In A. Andersen (Ed.), *Males with eating disorders* (pp. 77-98). New York: Brunner/Mazel.

Davis, C., & Cowles, M. (1989). A comparison of weight and diet concerns and personality factors among female athletes and non-athletes. *Journal of Psychosomatic Research, 33,* 527-536.

Dick, R.W. (1991). Eating disorders in NCAA athletic programs. *Athletic Training, 26*, 136-140.

Drewnowski, A., & Yee, D.K. (1987). Men and body image: Are males satisfied with their body weight? *Psychosomatic Medicine, 49*, 626-634.

Drinkwater, B.L., Bruemner, B., & Chesnut, C.H. (1990). Menstrual history as a determinant of current bone density in young athletes. *Journal of the American Medical Association, 263*, 545-548.

Drinkwater, B.L., Nilson, K., Chesnut, C.H., Bremner, W.J., Shainholtz, S., & Southworth, M.B. (1984). Bone mineral content of amenorrheic and eumenorrheic athletes. *New England Journal of Medicine, 311*, 277-281.

Dummer, G.M., Rosen, L.W., Heusner, W.W., Roberts, P.J., & Counsilman, J.E. (1987). Pathogenic weight-control behaviors of young competitive swimmers. *Physician and Sportsmedicine, 15*, 75-84.

Eisenman, P.A. (1990). Nutritional readiness. In J.L. Gabriel (Ed.), *U.S. Diving Safety Manual* (pp. 81-87). Indianapolis: U.S. Diving Publications.

Enns, M.P., Drewnowski, A., & Grinker, J.A. (1987). Body composition, body size estimation, and attitudes towards eating in male college athletes. *Psychosomatic Medicine, 49*, 56-64.

Epling, W.P., & Pierce, W.D. (1984). Activity-based anorexia in rats as a function of opportunity run on an activity wheel. *Nutrition and Behavior, 2*, 37-49.

Epling, W.P., & Pierce, W.D. (1988). Activity-based anorexia: A biobehavioral perspective. *International Journal of Eating Disorders, 7*, 475-485.

Epling, W.P., Pierce, W.D., & Stefan, L. (1981). Schedule-induced self-starvation. In C.M. Bradshaw, E. Szabadi, & C.F. Lowe (Eds.), *Quantification of steady-state operant behaviour* (pp. 393-396). Amsterdam: Elsevier/North Holland Biomedical Press.

Epling, W.P., Pierce, W.D., & Stefan, L. (1983). A theory of activity-based anorexia. *International Journal of Eating Disorders, 3*, 27-46.

Falls, H.B., & Humphrey, L.D. (1978). Body type and composition differences between placers and nonplacers in an AIAW gymnastics meet. *Research Quarterly, 49*, 38-43.

Frisch, R.E. (1977). Food intake, fatness, and reproductive ability. In R. Vigersky (Ed.), *Anorexia nervosa* (pp. 149-161). New York: Raven Press.

Frisch, R.E., & McArthur, J.W. (1974). Menstrual cycles: Fatness as a determinant of minimum weight for height necessary for their maintenance or onset. *Science, 185*, 949-951.

Frusztajer, N.T., Dhuper, S., Warren, M.P., Brooks-Gunn, J., & Fox, R.P. (1990). Nutrition and the incidence of stress fractures in ballet dancers. *American Journal of Clinical Nutrition, 51*, 779-783.

Gadpaille, W.J., Sanborn, C.F., & Wagner, W.W. (1987). Athletic amenorrhea, major affective disorders, and eating disorders. *American Journal of Psychiatry, 144*, 939-942.

Garfinkel, P.E., & Garner, D.M. (1982). *Anorexia nervosa: A multidimensional perspective*. New York: Brunner/Mazel.

Garfinkel, P.E., & Garner, D.M. (Eds.) (1987). *The role of drug treatments for eating disorders*. New York: Brunner/Mazel.

Garner, D.M. (1985). Iatrogenesis in anorexia nervosa and bulimia nervosa. *International Journal of Eating Disorders, 4*, 701-726.

Garner, D.M., & Garfinkel, P.E. (1979). The eating attitudes test: An index of the symptoms of anorexia nervosa. *Psychological Medicine, 9*, 273-279.

Garner, D.M., Garfinkel, P.E., Rockert, W., & Olmsted, M.P. (1987). A prospective study of eating disturbances in the ballet. *Psychotherapy and Psychosomatics, 48*, 170-175.

Garner, D.M., Olmsted, M.P., & Polivy, J. (1983). Development and validation of a multidimensional eating disorder inventory for anorexia nervosa and bulimia. *International Journal of Eating Disorders, 2*, 15-34.

Garner, D.M., & Rosen, L.W. (1991). Eating disorders among athletes: Research and recommendations. *Journal of Applied Sport Science Research, 5*, 100-107.

Grandjean, A.C. (1991). Eating disorders—the role of the athletic trainer. *Athletic Training, 26*, 105-112.

Gray, J.J., Ford, K., & Kelly, L.M. (1987). The prevalence of bulimia in a black college population. *International Journal of Eating Disorders, 6*, 733-740.

Halmi, K.A. (1991, November). *Ten year study: Anorexia nervosa*. Keynote address presented at the Tenth National Conference on Eating Disorders, Columbus, OH.

Hsu, L.K.G. (1987). Are the eating disorders becoming more common in blacks? *International Journal of Eating Disorders, 6*, 113-124.

Hsu, L.K.G. (1990). *Eating disorders*. New York: Guilford Press.

Johnson, C., & Connors, M. (1987). *The etiology and treatment of bulimia nervosa*. New York: Basic Books.

Kaplan, A.S., & Woodside, D.B. (1987). Biological aspects of anorexia nervosa and bulimia nervosa. *Journal of Consulting and Clinical Psychology, 55*, 645-653.

King, M.B., & Mezey, G. (1987). Eating behaviour of male racing jockeys. *Psychological Medicine, 17*, 249-253.

Lacey, J.H. (1990). Incest, incestuous fantasy and indecency: A clinical catchment area study of normal-weight bulimic women. *British Journal of Research, 157,* 399-403.

Lerner, R.M., & Karabenick, S.A. (1974). Physical attractiveness, body attitudes and self-concept in late adolescence. *Journal of Youth and Adolescence, 3,* 307-316.

Lerner, R.M., Orlos, J.B., & Knapp, J.R. (1976). Physical attractiveness, physical effectiveness, and self-concept in late adolescence. *Adolescence, 11,* 313-326.

Lissner, L., Odell, P.M., D'Agostino, R.B., Stokes, J., Kreger, B.E., Belanger, A.J., & Brownell, K.D. (1991). Variability of body weight and health outcomes in the Framingham population. *New England Journal of Medicine, 324,* 1839-1844.

Lundholm, J.K., & Littrell, J.M. (1986). Desire for thinness among high school cheerleaders: Relationship to disordered eating and weight control behaviors. *Adolescence, 21,* 573-579.

Mangi, R., Jokl, P., & Dayton, O.W. (1979). *The runner's complete medical guide.* New York: Summit Books.

Marcus, R., Cann, C., Madvig, P., Minkoff, J., Goddard, M., Bayer, M., Martin, M., Gaudiani, L., Haskell, W., & Genant, H. (1985). Menstrual function and bone mass in elite women distance runners. *Annals of Internal Medicine, 102,* 158-163.

McArthur, J.W., Bullen, B.A., Beitius, I.Z., Pagano, M., Badger, T.M., & Klibanski, A. (1980). Hypothalamic amenorrhea in runners of normal body composition. *Endocrinology Research Communications, 7,* 13-25.

McMurray, R.G., Ben-Ezra, V., Forsythe, W.A., & Smith, A.T. (1985). Responses of endurance-trained subjects to caloric deficits induced by diet or exercise. *Medicine and Science in Sports and Exercise, 17,* 574-579.

Mickalide, A.D. (1990). Sociocultural factors influencing weight among males. In A.E. Andersen (Ed.), *Males with eating disorders* (pp. 30-39). New York: Brunner/Mazel.

Mitchell, J.E. (1986). Anorexia nervosa: Medical and physiological aspects. In K.D. Brownell & J.P. Foreyt (Eds.), *Handbook of eating disorders* (pp. 247-265). New York: Basic Books.

Mitchell, J.E. (1990). *Bulimia nervosa.* Minneapolis: University of Minnesota Press.

Mitchell, J.E., & Eckert, E.D. (1987). Scope and significance of eating disorders. *Journal of Consulting and Clinical Psychology, 55,* 628-634.

Moffatt, R.J. (1984). Dietary status of elite female high school gymnasts: Inadequacy of vitamin and mineral intake. *Journal of the American Dietetic Association, 84,* 1361-1363.

Morgan, W.P., Brown, D.R., Raglin, J.S., O'Connor, P.J., & Ellickson, K.A. (1987). Psychological monitoring of overtraining and staleness. *British Journal of Sports Medicine, 21,* 107-114.

Moriarty, D., & Moriarty, M. (1991, October). *The incidence, detection, and treatment of eating disorders among athletes and fitness participants.* Paper presented at the Tenth National Conference on Eating Disorders, Columbus, OH.

National Collegiate Athletic Association. (1988). *Survey of NCAA member institutions and conferences on minority representation.* Unpublished survey.

National Collegiate Athletic Association. (1989). *Nutrition and eating disorders in college athletics.* Wilkes-Barre, PA: Karol Media.

Nudelman, S., Rosen, J.C., & Leitenberg, H. (1988). Dissimilarities in eating attitudes, body image distortion, depression and self-esteem between high-intensity male runners and women with bulimia nervosa. *International Journal of Eating Disorders, 7,* 625-634.

Oppenheimer, R., Howells, K., Palmer, R.L., & Chaloner, D.A. (1985). Adverse sexual experience in childhood and clinical eating disorders: A preliminary description. *Journal of Psychiatric Research, 19,* 357-361.

Orlick, T. (1990). *In pursuit of excellence* (2nd ed.). Champaign, IL: Leisure Press.

Owens, R.G., & Slade, P.D. (1987). Running and anorexia nervosa: An empirical study. *International Journal of Eating Disorders, 6,* 771-775.

Pasman, L., & Thompson, J.K. (1988). Body image and eating disturbance in obligatory runners, obligatory weightlifters, and sedentary individuals. *International Journal of Eating Disorders, 7,* 759-769.

Pavlou, K.N., Stefee, W.P., Lerman, R.H., & Burrows, B.A. (1985). Effects of dieting and exercise on lean body mass, oxygen uptake, and strength. *Medicine and Science in Sports and Exercise, 17,* 466-471.

Pierce, W.D., Epling, W.F., & Boer, D.P. (1986). Deprivation and satiation: The interrelations between food and wheel running. *Journal of the Experimental Analysis of Behavior, 46,* 199-210.

Polivy, J., & Herman, C.P. (1985). Dieting and binging: A causal analysis. *American Psychologist, 40,* 193-201.

Raglin, J.S. (1990). Exercise and mental health: Beneficial and detrimental effects. *Sports Medicine, 9,* 323-329.

Raglin, J.S. (in press). Overtraining and staleness: Psychometric monitoring of endurance athletes. In R. Singer, M. Murphy, &

K. Tennant (Eds.), *Handbook of research in sport psychology*. New York: Macmillan.

Rolls, B.J., Fedoroff, I.C., & Guthrie, J.F. (1991). Gender differences in eating behavior and body weight regulation. *Health Psychology, 10*, 133-142.

Root, M.P.P., Fallon, P., & Friedrich, W.N. (1986). *Bulimia: A systems approach to treatment*. New York: Norton.

Rosen, L.W., & Hough, D.O. (1988). Pathogenic weight-control behaviors of female college gymnasts. *Physician and Sportsmedicine, 16*, 141-144.

Rosen, L.W., McKeag, D.B., Hough, D.O., & Curley, V. (1986). Pathogenic weight-control behavior in female athletes. *Physician and Sportsmedicine, 14*, 79-86.

Rucinski, A. (1989). Relationship of body image and dietary intake of competitive ice skaters. *Journal of the American Dietetic Association, 89*, 98-100.

Ryan, R. (1991). Management of eating problems in athletic settings. In K. Brownell, J. Rodin, & J. Wilmore (Eds.), *Eating, body weight, and performance in athletes: Disorders of modern society* (pp. 344-362). Philadelphia: Lea & Febiger.

Sacks, M.H. (1990). Psychiatry and sport. *Annals of Sports Medicine, 5*, 47-52.

Schnitt, J.M., Schnitt, D., & Del A'une, W. (1986). Anorexia nervosa or thinness in modern dance students: Comparison with ballerinas. *Annals of Sports Medicine, 3*, 9-13.

Selby, R., Weinstein, H.M., & Bird, T.S. (1990). The health of university athletes: Attitudes, behaviors, and stressors. *Journal of American College Health, 39*, 11-18.

Sesan, R. (1989). Eating disorders and female athletes: A three-level intervention program. *Journal of College Student Development, 30*, 568-570.

Shangold, M., Rebar, R.W., Wentz, A.C., & Schiff, I. (1990). Evaluation and management of menstrual dysfunction in athletes. *Journal of the American Medical Association, 263*, 1665-1669.

Sherman, R.T., & Thompson, R.A. (1990). *Bulimia: A guide for family and friends*. Lexington, MA: Lexington Books.

Sherman, R.T., & Thompson, R.A. (1991). *Effects of race and thinness demand on prevalence of eating disturbance among women athletes*. Unpublished manuscript.

Shisslak, C.M., Crago, M., Neal, M.E., & Swain, B. (1987). Primary prevention of eating disorders. *Journal of Consulting and Clinical Psychology, 55*, 660-667.

Smith, N.J. (1984). Weight control in the athlete. *Clinics in Sports Medicine, 3*, 693-704.

Steen, S.N., & Brownell, K.D. (1990). Patterns of weight loss and regain in wrestlers: Has the tradition changed? *Medicine and Science in Sports and Exercise, 22*, 762-768.

Steen, S.N., & McKinney, S. (1986). Nutrition assessment of college wrestlers. *Physician and Sportsmedicine, 14*, 100-116.

Steen, S.N., Oppliger, R.A., & Brownell, K.D. (1988). Metabolic effects of repeated weight loss and regain in adolescent wrestlers. *Journal of the American Medical Association, 260*, 47-50.

Stephenson, J.N. (1991). Medical consequences and complications of anorexia nervosa and bulimia nervosa in female athletes. *Athletic Training, 26*, 130-135.

Strauss, R.H., Lanese, R.R., & Malarkey, W.B. (1985). Weight loss in amateur wrestlers and its effects on serum testosterone levels. *Journal of the American Medical Association, 254*, 3337-3338.

Strober, M. (1986). Anorexia nervosa: History and psychological concepts. In K.D. Brownell & J.P. Foreyt (Eds.), *Handbook of eating disorders* (pp. 231-246). New York: Basic Books.

Szmukler, G.I., Eisler, I., Gillies, C., & Hayward, M.E. (1985). The implications of anorexia nervosa in a ballet school. *Journal of Psychiatric Research, 19*, 177-181.

Thompson, R. (1987). Management of the athlete with an eating disorder: Implications for the sport management team. *The Sport Psychologist, 1*, 114-126.

Thompson, R.A., & Sherman, R.T. (1989). Therapist errors in treating eating disorders: Relationship and process. *Psychotherapy, 26*, 62-68.

Tipton, C.M., Tcheng, T.K., & Paul, W.D. (1969). Evaluation of the Hall method for determining minimum wrestling weights. *Journal of the Iowa Medical Society, 59*, 571-574.

United States Olympic Committee. (1987). *Sports nutrition: Weight loss and sports performance*. Colorado Springs: U.S. Olympic Committee.

Vandereycken, W., & Meermann, R. (1984). Anorexia nervosa: Is prevention possible? *International Journal of Psychiatry in Medicine, 14*, 191-205.

Waldholtz, B.D., & Andersen, A.E. (1990). Gastrointestinal symptoms in anorexia nervosa. *Gastroenterology, 98*, 1415-1419.

Warren, M.P. (1983). Physical and biological aspects of puberty. In J. Brooks-Gunn & A.C. Petersen (Eds.), *Girls at puberty: Biological and psychosocial perspectives* (pp. 3-28). New York: Plenum.

Warren, M.P., Brooks-Gunn, J., Hamilton, L.H., Warren, L.F., & Hamilton, W.G. (1986). Scoliosis and fractures in young ballet dancers: Relation to delayed menarche and secondary amenorrhea. *New England Journal of Medicine, 314*, 1348-1353.

Webster, S., Rutt, R., & Weltman, A. (1990). Physiological effects of a weight loss regimen practiced by college wrestlers. *Medicine and Science in Sports and Exercise, 22*, 229-233.

Weight, L.M., & Noakes, T.D. (1987). Is running an analog of anorexia? A survey of the incidence of eating disorders in female distance runners. *Medicine and Science in Sports and Exercise, 19*, 213-217.

Whitney, E.N., & Hamilton, E.M.N. (1984). *Understanding nutrition* (3rd ed.). St. Paul: West Publishing.

Wilkins, J.A., Boland, F.J., & Albinson, J. (1991). A comparison of male and female university athletes and nonathletes on eating disorder indices: Are athletes protected? *Journal of Sport Behavior, 14*, 129-143.

Wilmore, J.H., Brown, C.II., & Davis, J.A. (1977). Body physique and composition of the female distance runner. *Annals of the New York Academy of Science, 301*, 764-776.

Wilmore, J.H., & Costill, D.L. (1987). *Training for sport and activity: The physiological basis of the conditioning process* (3rd ed.). Boston: Allyn & Bacon.

Wilson, C.A., Abdenour, T.E., & Keye, W.R. (1991). Menstrual disorders among intercollegiate athletes and non-athletes: Perceived impact on performance. *Athletic Training, 26*, 170-177.

Wolf, E.M.B., Wirth, J.C., & Lohman, T.G. (1979). Nutritional practices of coaches in the Big Ten. *Physician and Sportsmedicine, 7*, 112-124.

Woodside, D.B., Garner, D.M., Rockert, W., & Garfinkel, P.E. (1990). Eating disorders in males: Insights from a clinical and psychometric comparison with female patients. In A. Andersen (Ed.), *Males with eating disorders* (pp. 100-115). New York: Brunner/Mazel.

Yates, A. (1991). *Compulsive exercise and the eating disorders.* New York: Brunner/Mazel.

Yates, A., Leehey, K., & Shisslak, C.M. (1983). Running—an analog of anorexia? *New England Journal of Medicine, 308*, 251-255.

Index